The European Union since 1945

SEMINAR STUDIES   IN HISTORY

The European Union since 1945

ALASDAIR BLAIR

PEARSON
Longman

Harlow, England • London • New York • Boston • San Francisco • Toronto
Sydney • Tokyo • Singapore • Hong Kong • Seoul • Taipei • New Delhi
Cape Town • Madrid • Mexico City • Amsterdam • Munich • Paris • Milan

PEARSON EDUCATION LIMITED

Edinburgh Gate
Harlow CM20 2JE
United Kingdom
Tel: +44 (0)1279 623623
Fax: +44 (0)1279 431059
Website: www.pearsoned.co.uk

First edition published in Great Britain in 2005

© Pearson Education Limited 2005

The right of Alasdair Blair to be identified as author
of this work has been asserted by him in accordance
with the Copyright, Designs and Patents Act 1988.

ISBN   978-0-582-42393-0

British Library Cataloguing in Publication Data
A CIP catalogue record for this book can be obtained from the British Library

Library of Congress Cataloging in Publication Data
Blair, Alasdair, 1971–
     The European Union since 1945 / Alasdair Blair.—1st ed.
        p. cm. — (Seminar studies in history)
     Includes bibliographical references and index.
     ISBN 0–582–42393–7 (pbk.)
     1. European Union—History. 2. European federation—History. I. Title. II. Series.

JN30.B62 2005
341.242'2—dc22

2004043180

10   9   8   7   6   5
09   08   07

Set by 35 in 10/12.5pt Sabon
Printed and bound in Malaysia, VVP

The Publisher's policy is to use paper manufactured from sustainable forests.

For William

CONTENTS

INTRODUCTION TO THE SERIES

Such is the pace of historical enquiry in the modern world that there is an ever-widening gap between the specialist article or monograph, incorporating the results of current research, and general surveys, which inevitably become out of date. *Seminar Studies in History* is designed to bridge this gap. The series was founded by Patrick Richardson in 1966 and his aim was to cover major themes in British, European and World history. Between 1980 and 1996 Roger Lockyer continued his work, before handing the editorship over to Clive Emsley and Gordon Martel. Clive Emsley is Professor of History at the Open University, while Gordon Martel is Professor of International History at the University of Northern British Columbia, Canada, and Senior Research Fellow at De Montfort University.

All the books are written by experts in their field who are not only familiar with the latest research but have often contributed to it. They are frequently revised, in order to take account of new information and interpretations. They provide a selection of documents to illustrate major themes and provoke discussion, and also a guide to further reading. The aim of *Seminar Studies in History* is to clarify complex issues without over-simplifying them, and to stimulate readers into deepening their knowledge and understanding of major themes and topics.

ACKNOWLEDGEMENTS

The publishers are grateful to the following for permission to reproduce copyright material:

Pearson Education for Maps 1–6, adapted from *The Longman Companion to the European Union since 1945* by Alasdair Blair © Alasdair Blair, 1999.

In some instances we have been unable to trace the owners of copyright material, and we would appreciate any information that would enable us to do so.

Map 1 The Six member states (1957)

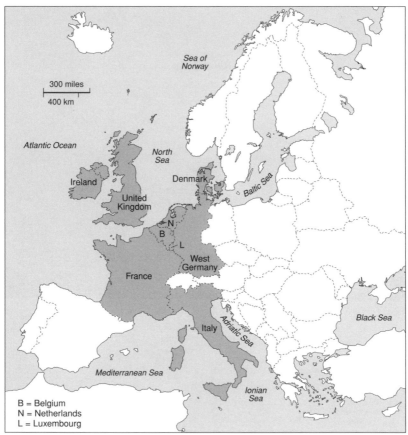

Map 2 The Nine member states (1973)

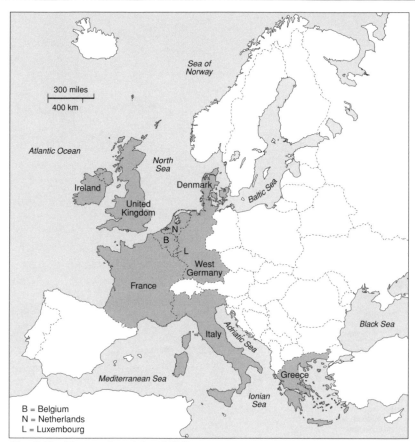

Map 3 The Ten member states (1981)

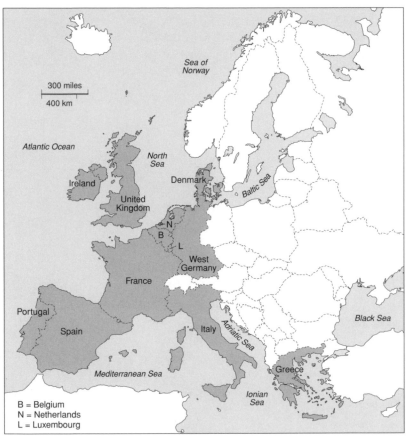

Map 4 The Twelve member states (1986)

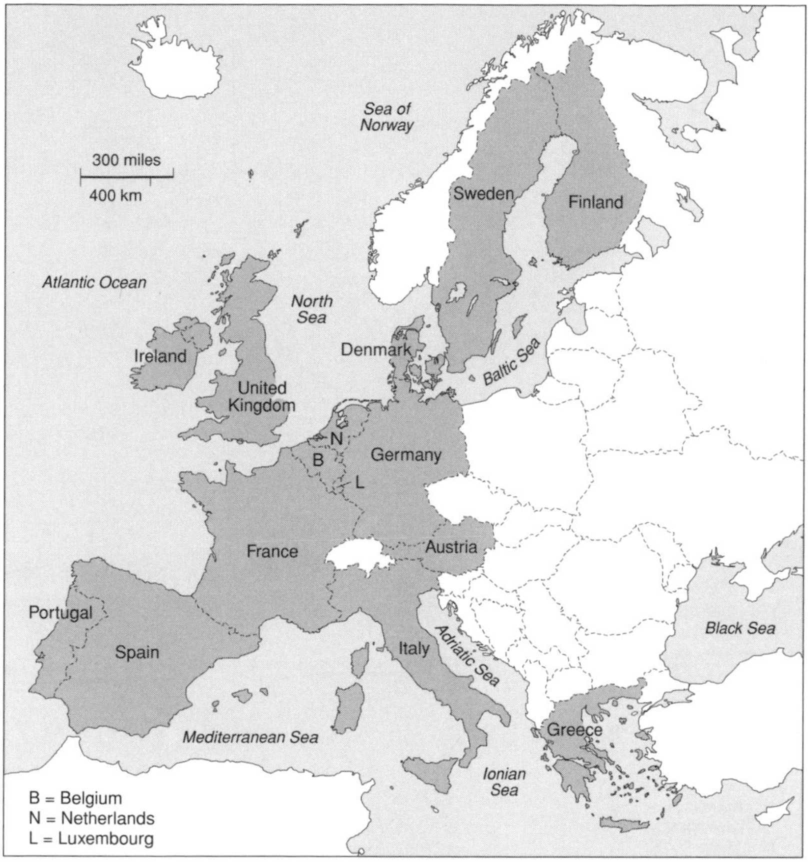

Map 5 The Fifteen member states (1995)

Within the map:
- Sea of Norway
- 300 miles / 400 km
- Sweden
- Finland
- Atlantic Ocean
- North Sea
- Ireland
- Denmark
- Baltic Sea
- United Kingdom
- N
- B
- Germany
- L
- France
- Austria
- Portugal
- Black Sea
- Spain
- Italy
- Adriatic Sea
- Mediterranean Sea
- Greece
- Ionian Sea

B = Belgium
N = Netherlands
L = Luxembourg

Map 6 The Twenty-Five member states and applicant countries (2004)

PREFACE

This book is not of course a work of original research but draws heavily on the work of others. The aim of the book is to provide an accessible introduction to the study of European integration. It is a subject matter that is often confused by terminology. The Treaties of Rome created two communities: a European Economic Community (EEC) and a European Atomic Energy Community (Euratom). In 1967 they merged with the European Coal and Steel Community (ECSC) to form a single institutional structure. From the 1970s onwards it was commonplace to refer to all three institutions as the European Community (EC). I have therefore used the term EEC up until the end of the 1960s and from then on the term EC. This is despite the fact that the EEC was not officially renamed the EC until the 1993 Maastricht Treaty on European Union. At this point the EC became a separate entity of the European Union (EU) that was created by the Maastricht Treaty and I therefore use the term EU from 1993 onwards. On occasion, I have adopted the practice of referring to the EEC/EC/EU simply as 'Europe' as this is the term that is often used in debates on the subject.

In writing this book a great many friends and colleagues have shared their thoughts with me and have had an important impact on the outcome. I would particularly like to thank Professor Catherine Hoskyns and Dr Alex Kazamias of Coventry University and Professor John Young of Nottingham University, who were kind enough to comment on draft chapters of the book. I am also indebted to the editing skills of Simon Kear, whose efforts greatly improved the clarity of the text. I would additionally like to thank Coventry University students who took courses on the EU and who to varying degrees were exposed to and assisted with the material that is contained within this book. Special thanks are due to the financial support of the European Commission Jean Monnet scheme. I am particularly indebted to the kind encouragement and extreme patience of the series editors, especially Professor Gordon Martel. Thanks are also due to Casey Mein who served as my publisher at Longman. Finally, and not least, my thanks and love to Katherine for her support, and to our son William for providing plenty of welcome diversions from this work. I hardly need say that none of these individuals bears the slightest responsibility for the book's remaining deficiencies.

Alasdair Blair, Thornton, August 2004

ABBREVIATIONS

Benelux	Benelux Economic Union (Belgium, the Netherlands and Luxembourg)
CAP	Common Agricultural Policy
CFSP	Common Foreign and Security Policy
Comecon	Council for Mutual Economic Assistance
CoR	The Committee of the Regions
Coreper	Committee of Permanent Representatives
EBRD	European Bank for Reconstruction and Development
EC	European Community
ECB	European Central Bank
ECJ	European Court of Justice
ECSC	European Coal and Steel Community
ECU	European Currency Unit
EDC	European Defence Community
EEA	European Economic Area
EEC	European Economic Community
EFTA	European Free Trade Association
EMI	European Monetary Institute
EMS	European Monetary System
EMU	Economic and Monetary Union
EPC	European Political Cooperation
ERDF	European Regional Development Fund
ERM	Exchange Rate Mechanism
ESCB	European System of Central Banks
ESDI	European Security and Defence Identity
ESPRIT	European Strategic Programme for Research and Development in Information Technology
EU	European Union
Euratom	European Atomic Energy Community
GATT	General Agreement on Tariffs and Trade
GDP	Gross domestic product
GNP	Gross national product
IGC	Intergovernmental conference
JHA	Justice and home affairs

MEP	Member of the European Parliament
NATO	North Atlantic Treaty Organisation
OECD	Organisation for Economic Cooperation and Development
OEEC	Organisation for European Economic Cooperation
QMV	Qualified majority voting
SEA	Single European Act
SEM	Single European Market
TEU	Treaty on European Union
UEF	European Union of Federalists
USA	United States of America
WEU	Western European Union
WTO	World Trade Organisation

THE ENLARGEMENT OF THE EU

The Six 1957	The Nine 1973	The Ten 1981	The Twelve 1986	The Fifteen 1995	The Twenty-Five 2004	Applicant countries
Belgium	Britain	Greece	Portugal	Austria	Cyprus	Bulgaria
France	Denmark		Spain	Finland	Czech Republic	Romania
West Germany	Ireland			Sweden	Estonia	Turkey
Italy					Hungary	
Luxembourg					Latvia	
Netherlands					Lithuania	
					Malta	
					Poland	
					Slovakia	
					Slovenia	

CHRONOLOGY

1945

February	Yalta conference dealing with questions relating to the postwar settlement.
July–August	Potsdam conference on postwar settlement.

1946

5 March	Winston Churchill's 'iron curtain' speech.
19 September	Winston Churchill's 'United States of Europe' speech.
December	Formation of the European Union of Federalists (UEF)

1947

4 March	Treaty of Dunkirk.
12 March	Truman Doctrine.
5 June	Marshall Plan announced.

1948

January	Benelux customs union established.
17 March	Signature of Brussels Treaty (collective alliance of Britain, France and Benelux).
16 April	Organisation for European Economic Cooperation (OEEC) created to coordinate the Marshall Plan for West European countries.
7–11 May	Movement for European unity held European Congress in The Hague.
24 June	Commencement of Berlin blockade.

1949

4 April	Creation of North Atlantic Treaty Organisation (NATO).
5 May	Council of Europe founded.

1950

9 May	Publication of Schuman Declaration.

20 June	Start of negotiations to establish the European Coal and Steel Community (ECSC) as 'a first step in the federation of Europe'.
24 October	Pleven Plan for a European Defence Community (EDC).

1951

15 February	Commencement of negotiations to establish a European Defence Community.
18 April	European Coal and Steel Community Treaty signed by Belgium, France, Germany, Italy, Luxembourg and the Netherlands (the Six).

1952

27 May	EDC Treaty signed by 'the Six' in Paris. Treaty of Association signed with UK.
27 July	ECSC came into operation.

1954

30 August	French National Assembly rejected the European Defence Community Treaty.
23 October	Brussels Treaty amended to create the Western European Union.

1955

5 May	Germany joined NATO.
2–4 June	Messina Conference of 'the Six' foreign ministers established the Spaak Committee.

1956

June	Start of negotiations to establish a European Economic Community (EEC) and European Atomic Energy Community (Euratom).
31 October	Franco–British intervention in the Suez Canal.

1957

25 March	Signing of the Treaties of Rome which established the EEC and Euratom.

1958

1 January	The Treaties of Rome came into effect, thereby launching the EEC and Euratom.
7 January	Walter Hallstein appointed the first President of the European Commission.

1959

1 January   First tariff reductions in the common market.

1960

3 May   Creation of European Free Trade Association (EFTA) by
                   Austria, Denmark, Norway, Portugal, Sweden, Switzerland and
                   the UK.

14 December   Organisation for Economic Cooperation and Development
                   (OECD) established, replacing the OEEC.

1961

July–August   Denmark, Ireland and the UK applied for EEC membership.

2 November   Publication of the Fouchet Plan for a European political
                   community.

1962

14 January   Common agricultural policy (CAP) agreed by the Six.

17 April   Collapse of the Fouchet Plan negotiations.

1963

14 January   French President General Charles de Gaulle vetoed Britain's
                   application to join the Community.

22 January   Franco–German Treaty of Friendship.

20 July   The Yaoundé Convention signed, consisting of an association
                   of 18 African states and Madagascar with the EEC for five
                   years.

1964

4 May   Start of the Kennedy round of General Agreement on Tariffs
                   and Trade (GATT) negotiations, with the EEC taking a leading
                   role.

1965

8 April   Merger Treaty brought the ECSC, Euratom and the EEC into
                   a common institutional format (the European Communities)
                   with effect from 1 July 1967.

1 July   Commencement of the empty chair crisis when France boycotted
                   all meetings of the Council of Ministers.

1966

29 January   Luxembourg Compromise resolved the empty chair crisis.

1967

2 May	Britain reapplied to join the Community, to be followed by Ireland and Denmark and, a little later, Norway.
1 July	Merger of the Community Executives (ECSC High Authority, EEC and Euratom Commissions) into one 14-member Commission.
27 November	French President Charles de Gaulle stressed the incompatibility of the British economy and the EEC, which brought to an end Britain's second membership application.

1968

1 July	Customs union completed 18 months ahead of schedule.

1969

28 April	Resignation of French President Charles de Gaulle. Succeeded in July by Georges Pompidou.
1–2 December	The Six agreed to complete, enlarge and strengthen the Community at 'the Hague summit'.

1970

7–8 October	Werner Report set out a plan to achieve economic and monetary union.
27 October	Establishment of European Political Cooperation (EPC) for foreign policy coordination.
19 November	First EPC meeting took place in Munich.

1971

1 January	Second Yaoundé and Arusha Conventions came into force.
22 March	Member states agreed on a plan to achieve Economic and Monetary Union (EMU) by 1980 (not achieved because of difficulties in the international economy).

1972

21 March	Introduction of the currency 'snake' which formed the exchange rate agreement between Belgium, France, Germany, Italy and the Netherlands.
24–25 September	Norway withdrew its application to join the Community after a Norwegian referendum showed a majority against entry.
19–20 October	The Paris summit of the Nine prepared a blueprint for the future development of the Community. It was the very first summit meeting of the heads of state and government of the future enlarged Community of the Nine (Belgium, France, Germany,

Italy, Luxembourg, the Netherlands, Denmark, Ireland and the
United Kingdom).

1973

1 January   Accession of Denmark, Ireland and the UK to the EEC.

1974

4 June   Britain outlined details of its terms of renegotiation of EEC
                     membership.

9–10 December   The Paris summit agreed to the principle of direct elections to the
                     European Parliament and the institutionalisation of summit
                     meetings by means of establishing the European Council.

1975

28 February   The Lomé Convention signed, constituting an agreement between
                     the EEC and 46 underdeveloped countries in Africa, the
                     Caribbean and Pacific (ACP countries). It replaced and extended
                     the 1963 and 1969 Yaoundé Conventions and the Arusha
                     Agreement.

18 March   European Regional Development Fund (ERDF) established.

5 June   UK referendum on EC membership – 17.3 million voted 'yes'
                     to stay in the EEC, 8.4 million voted 'no' to withdraw.

29 December   Tindemans Report on political cooperation presented to member
                     states, having been called for at the 1974 Paris summit.

1978

6–7 July   European Council summit in Bremen approved the
                     Franco–German plan to establish the European Monetary
                     System (EMS).

1979

9–10 March   European Council meeting in Paris brought the EMS into
                     operation.

7–10 June   First direct elections to the European Parliament.

31 October   The second Lomé Convention (Lomé II) signed between the EEC
                     and the 58 ACP states.

1981

1 January   Greece became the tenth member of the European Community.

6–12 November   Genscher-Colombo initiative to further develop European
                     political cooperation by creating a common foreign policy and
                     the coordination of security policy.

1984

1 January	Creation of EEC–EFTA free trade area.
14 February	European Parliament adopted the Draft Treaty establishing the European Union.
14–17 June	Second direct elections to the European Parliament.
25–26 June	Fontainebleau European Council produced agreement on the UK budget rebate.
8 December	Third Lomé Convention signed.

1985

7 January	Jacques Delors took office as head of a new European Commission.
9 March	The Dooge committee recommended the convening of an intergovernmental conference to examine the reform of the Treaty of Rome.
14 June	Schengen agreement. Belgium, France, Germany, Luxembourg and the Netherlands reached agreement on the gradual abolition of frontier controls.
15 June	Lord Cockfield presented his timetable for the completion of the internal market.
28–29 June	Milan European Council meeting approved the European Commission's project to complete the internal market. The meeting also established an intergovernmental conference to look at the wider reform of the Treaty.
2–3 December	Luxembourg European Council reached agreement on the Single European Act (SEA), which reformed the Treaties of Rome.

1986

1 January	Portugal and Spain joined the Community.
February	Foreign ministers signed the Single European Act.

1987

1 July	Single European Act came into existence.

1988

27–28 June	EEC member states agreed at the Hanover European Council to establish the Delors committee on Economic and Monetary Union.

1989

12 April	Delors Report proposed a three-stage route to EMU: linking the currencies, integration between states and the creation of a European Central Bank (ECB).

2000

March   Lisbon European Council produced agreement on an approach to assist economic modernisation.

7–9 December   Nice European Council marked the conclusion of the intergovernmental conference negotiations that started in Brussels in February 2000.

2001

2 January   Greece became the 12th member of the euro zone.

June   Ireland rejected the Treaty of Nice in a referendum.

11 September   Terrorist attacks on the United States resulted in the collapse of the World Trade Centre building in New York and spurred the US into a 'war against terrorism'.

2002

1 January   Changeover to the use of euro banknotes and coins and the withdrawal of national banknotes and coins.

February   Convention on the Future of Europe began in Brussels.

28 February   End of the period of dual circulation of currencies and the euro therefore became the sole currency within the 12 participating member states of the euro zone.

31 May   The EU ratified the Kyoto Protocol on climate change.

June   The ECSC came to an end (after 50 years in existence).

2003

1 February   Treaty of Nice came into effect.

20–21 June   Thessalonica European Council meeting in Greece discussed the draft Constitutional Treaty produced by the Convention on the Future of Europe that was chaired by Valery Giscard d'Estaing and which commenced work in February 2002.

14 September   The Swedish electorate rejected the euro in a referendum vote.

4 October   The IGC negotiations on the Future of Europe commenced in Rome under the leadership of the Italian presidency of the European Union.

12 December   At the Brussels European Council it was agreed that it was not possible for the IGC negotiations that had commenced on 4 October 2003 to reach an overall agreement on a draft constitutional treaty.

2004

25–26 March   Brussels European Council discussed the progress of the IGC negotiations and noted the commitment of member states to

	agree on the Constitutional Treaty before the June European Council meeting. Member states also adopted a Declaration on Combating Terrorism in the wake of the terrorist train bomb attacks in Madrid on 11 March.
29 March	Bulgaria, Estonia, Latvia, Lithuania, Romania, Slovakia and Slovenia became full NATO members.
1 May	Cyprus, the Czech Republic, Estonia, Hungary, Latvia, Lithuania, Malta, Poland, Slovakia and Slovenia became members of the European Union, which now totalled 25 member states.
10–13 June	Sixth direct elections to the European Parliament held in 25 member states.
17–18 June	Brussels European Council reached agreement on the EU Constitution.
29 June	At Brussels Council meeting of heads of state or government it was agreed that José Manuel Durão Barroso would be nominated as the successor to Romano Prodi as President of the Commission. It was also agreed that Javier Solana would be appointed as Secretary-General of the Council and High Representative for CFSP and that on the day of entry into force of the EU Constitution he would be appointed EU Minister for Foreign Affairs.

PART ONE   BACKGROUND

CHAPTER ONE

THE PROBLEM OF EUROPEAN INTEGRATION

On the afternoon of 9 May 1950 in the elaborate clock room of the French foreign ministry in Paris, the French Foreign Minister, Robert Schuman, proposed the creation of an organisation that would take responsibility for Franco-German coal and steel production [Doc.9]. Barely five years after the end of the Second World War, the Declaration aimed to link the interests of European states by establishing a common organisation to oversee coal and steel production. The choice of coal and steel was deliberate because they represented the most important economic industries at the time and were the basis for military power. More than five decades later, observers may find it difficult to understand the true significance of the proposals that Schuman advanced: not only did they provide a structure to unite countries that had spent much of the previous century at war with each other, but they represented a departure from the tactics employed after the First World War when French attempts to suppress German power had failed.

Schuman's plans were attractive to France and Germany for different reasons. For France, they offered the prospect of leadership in Europe and a method of controlling (but not suppressing) Germany. For Germany, they offered the chance to cleanse the horrors of the Third Reich and to be treated as an equal partner with other European countries. Apart from the support of France and Germany, Schuman's proposals were warmly received in the capitals of Belgium, Italy, Luxembourg and the Netherlands and resulted in 'the six' countries agreeing on 18 April 1951 to establish a European Coal and Steel Community (ECSC) which eventually came into operation on 25 July 1952. Five years later, in March 1957, the same six countries signed the Treaties of Rome that created the European Economic Community (EEC) and European Atomic Energy Community (Euratom) [Doc.15].

In the years that have passed, numerous reforms and changes have enhanced the influence of the institutions that govern the European Union (EU) of today. There has also taken place an expansion of membership, from the six states of the ECSC to the 25 member states of the EU [Doc.38]. At the same time, there has occurred a growth in the number of policies that are now tackled at the EU level, from matters relating to consumer affairs and the environment to international trade policy and the single currency. And although some of these developments have been the product of incremental change over the last five decades (since 1950), a great many more have been undertaken in the period since 1990. There has therefore been a considerable quickening in the pace of European integration in recent times, as evidenced by the creation of the single currency and the fact that the EU's membership has more than doubled in the ten years from 1994 to 2004. As a consequence, more and more decisions that were once taken at the national level are now taken at a European level, involving the input of the supranational institutions of the European Commission and European Parliament as well as the member states in the form of the Council of Ministers. Member states are also faced with the impact of European law that has supremacy over national law.

Some individuals may conclude that the cumulative effect of these changes has been an unacceptable transfer of power away from national governments and a reduction in national sovereignty that can be rectified only by a member state withdrawing from the EU. Such a course of action is influenced by claims that the costs of EU membership for some member states, such as Britain, outweigh the benefits. In crude terms, they pay in more money than they get out. It is an argument that was used to considerable effect by the UK Independence Party in the 2004 European Parliament elections, when they obtained 11 out of a total of 78 UK MEPs. The simplicity of this argument responds to fears among the electorate that interference from 'Brussels' has led to unnecessary legislation that would not otherwise be implemented if it had been left to a national government to decide on an individual basis. Such an argument does, however, fail to address the negative implication that withdrawal would have on business competitiveness and employment levels. Many more critics of European integration do, nevertheless, appreciate that certain benefits accrue from membership. This principally constitutes the ability to trade and move freely within Europe, while initiatives that seek to deepen European integration into other policy areas are steadfastly resisted.

In contrast to these viewpoints, many other individuals consider that the EU does not possess enough power, influence and resources for it to be able to effectively deal with the challenges that it faces. The argument here is that the series of negotiations which have shaped the EU have been determined by the need to achieve compromise and as such the EU's influence and abilities have often been deliberately limited to appease member state concern.

As ever, there is an element of truth in each of these categorisations. On the one hand, EU rules can at times appear to be overly burdensome, and yet at the same time it has often appeared to be ill equipped to deal with the challenges it has faced. Beneath these differing views is the greater reality that the EU's structure and scope of policy competences have essentially been the product of the decisions taken by member state governments. The member state governments agreed to all the reforms that enhanced the powers of the European Parliament in the Single European Act, Treaty on European Union, Treaty of Amsterdam and Treaty of Nice. Similarly, the expansion in the European Commission's responsibility into matters relating to the single market, and the agreement to make greater use of the majority voting procedure within the Council of Ministers, were also judged to be appropriate developments by member state governments.

This evidence of member states acting as the key decision-maker contrasts with the initial views held by Robert Schuman (French Foreign Minister from 1948–53) and Jean Monnet (who in 1946 had been appointed head of the French Planning Commission by de Gaulle to oversee France's economic recovery). They argued that once member states had enjoyed the benefits of integration in one area they would inevitably agree to extend cooperation into other policy areas. According to this idea of spillover, the experience of integrating coal and steel industries would in time lead to the joining together of defence industries which would in turn forge the creation of a common foreign and defence policy. But integration has been neither inevitable nor automatic. This was initially demonstrated by the collapse of the European Defence Community (EDC) in 1954 [*Doc.12*]. A decade later, France's refusal to accept European Commission proposals to enhance the powers of European Parliament and extend the use of qualified majority voting (QMV) resulted in the government in Paris refusing to take part in meetings of the Council of Ministers in the second half of 1965. This period, which is referred to as the empty chair crisis, directly led to the Luxembourg compromise of January 1966 which cemented the position of member states and limited the opportunity for further European integration until the mid-1980s [*Doc.20*]. Thus, as I argue in this book, moves towards the taking of decisions at a European level and the transfer of power away from member states have been primarily the result of the pragmatic decisions of member states.

In taking such a path, member state governments have for the most part concluded that a fundamental benefit of European integration has been the ability to tackle problems that could not be adequately dealt with by any one individual state. Hence, in the postwar period many countries were willing to engage in new forms of cooperation and to create supranational structures to administer common policies purely because they considered that individual governments were not able to cope with the challenges that Western Europe faced. In examining the factors that motivated states to engage in such a process of integration, Alan Milward has emphasised the point that the creation of the ECSC represented a desire to satisfy French national interests by ensuring the continued economic recovery of France (Milward, 1984). Germany was equally keen to participate in the ECSC (as was Italy) because it provided a means of rehabilitation, while the smaller nations of Belgium, Luxembourg and the Netherlands realised that they could not economically afford to distance themselves from the markets of France and Germany. A number of years later, the British government concluded that the economic benefits of participating in the EEC far outweighed the impact that integration would have on national sovereignty. This focus on the national interest has led Milward to argue that European integration took place only when it was demanded by nation states and that supranational institutions were established for specific purposes and not as a means of eclipsing the nation state (Milward, 1992).

A casual observer might be forgiven for thinking that a cumulative effect of over 50 years of European integration and the continued desire of countries to join the EU would be reflected in the Union having a high degree of popularity within the member states. One might also conclude that the experience of doing business with each other would produce a convergence of views among the member states. Yet for both questions the opposite has been the case. Eurosceptic causes have taken hold in all member states, while there additionally appears to be a decline in interest in European affairs among the electorate. Thus, the average level of voting fell for the sixth time running at the June 2004 European Parliamentary elections, with voting being particularly poor in the countries of Central and Eastern Europe that had joined the EU only a matter of weeks earlier [*Doc.40*].

This, of course, raises the question as to the reasons for such an outcome. Are low turnouts in European elections the result of voter apathy? Does the electorate appreciate the many benefits of EU membership? Or is it simply the case that we should not be surprised by the lack of support for and awareness of European integration? In this sense, should we just accept the fact that the transfer of power away from member states is likely to be greeted with concerns about the erosion of sovereignty among a national electorate that continue in their eyes to be governed and influenced by law and policies that are shaped within a member state? Key policies such as taxation and education continue to be set by national governments, while up till now a European army or police force has not been created. Yet, at the same time, a great number of decisions which affect member states are taken at the EU level, such as in the area of social affairs. Thus, European citizens are presented with a picture that highlights the continued influence of member states and at the same time the erosion in their ability to individually determine many policies. It is a confusing picture that raises a number of important questions. Why have member states been willing to share the responsibility for taking decisions with other member states? Why have particular member states, such as Britain, been more reluctant to support EU membership than others? What are the implications of some member states participating in certain policy areas while others choose not?

The preceding summary provides a superficial examination of some of the key issues and questions that concern the study of European integration.

Nevertheless, students may begin to appreciate the complex nature of the study of the European Union. The chapters that follow provide an overview of the history of European integration without entering into the blow-by-blow account that would be impossible in such a concise book. Readers are therefore encouraged to consult the other studies that are listed at the end of the book for more detailed explanations of the policies and personalities that are highlighted in this text.

PART TWO   ANALYSIS

CHAPTER TWO

THE ROAD TO ROME: 1945–57

THE EMERGENCE OF EUROPEAN UNITY

Despite the fact that the ideal of European unity was overwhelmingly influenced by the impact of the Second World War, the plan of a united Europe that overcame national jealousies was not a new idea. In the inter-war years of 1918–39 a number of plans were produced that sought to create new forms of cooperation among European nations. This included the Pan-European Union that was founded in 1923 by the Austrian Count Richard Coudenhove-Kalergi, who had argued the previous year for the creation of a European federation in his book *Paneuropa*. In the aftermath of the devastating impact of the First World War, the Pan-European Union acquired a loyal following that included individuals who shaped European integration in the post-1945 era – such as Konrad Adenauer and Georges Pompidou – as well as leading politicians of the time. The latter included Aristide Briand, who, as French Foreign Minister, proposed a scheme to create a confederal bond between European states at the League of Nations in September 1929. Some months later, these ideas were outlined in the Briand Memorandum of 1 May 1930. It argued that European governments should establish a union within the structure of the League of Nations and would include the creation of a permanent political committee and supporting secretariat [*Doc.1*]. But despite the historical significance of Briand's proposals, there was a conspicuous lack of support from other leading European nations. The lack of interest from the likes of Britain, Germany and Italy, combined with Briand's death in March 1932, brought to an end the proposals that had been outlined in the Briand Memorandum.

The remainder of the 1930s saw little progress towards European unity and it would take the horrors of the Second World War to revive interest in European integration. The Free French, led by General Charles de Gaulle, expressed an interest in some form of European cooperation, with de Gaulle inviting Europeans on 11 November 1942 'to join together in a practical and lasting fashion'. Nearly two years later, the leaders of Belgium, Luxembourg and the Netherlands announced in September 1944 that they wished to establish a Benelux customs union (eventually established in January 1948). These initiatives were greatly influenced by the wartime resistance movement which concluded that peace could be secured only through the creation of some form of European framework. This directly led to the formation in December 1946 of the European Union of Federalists (Européenne des Fedéralistes) which argued for the creation of a United States of Europe and the creation of a constitution for this purpose.

Over and above all other factors, European integration in the postwar period was shaped by two key developments. The first was the emerging cold war bipolar division of Europe that had been emphasised by the agreement reached at the Yalta summit of 1945 to divide Europe into 'spheres of influence', a policy which had itself initially been reflected in the October 1944 agreement in which Churchill and Stalin agreed to a 50:50 division of Yugoslavia and a 90:10 division of Greece in Britain's favour. But while the Western Allies viewed the division of Europe to be a temporary affair, it rapidly became apparent that the Soviet Union regarded the division to be a permanent fixture and ensured that governments favourable to its interests were installed in those countries that fell within its sphere of influence. The reality of this state of affairs prompted Winston Churchill to observe in his March 1946 speech at Fulton, Missouri that 'an iron curtain has descended across the [European] continent' [*Doc.2*]. Some months later, in September 1946, Churchill spoke of the need to 'build a kind of United States of Europe' around a Franco-German axis to provide a structure to promote peace and stability [*Doc.3*]. The second key factor concerned the need to tackle the dire economic situation that affected European nations as a result of the war having inflicted massive infrastructure damage that had obliterated houses, factories and roads. This difficult economic situation also impacted on the ability of European nations to defend themselves, a factor that was emphasised in February 1947 when an exhausted Britain was no longer capable of providing support to Greece at a time when the government in Athens was seriously threatened by the attempts of Communist guerrillas to take power.

The combination of Europe's difficult economic situation and the threat posed by the Soviet Union produced a swift American response. In March 1947 US President Harry Truman pledged America's support for 'free peoples who are resisting subjugation by armed minorities or by outside pressures'. The Truman Doctrine, as it came to be known, marked the start of a more active US foreign policy, where Western Europe was the most immediate beneficiary. Yet an exhausted Europe was not only incapable of defending itself from the Soviet threat, it was also unable to support itself in terms of its food requirements. The stark reality of the dire economic situation that faced Europe was not lost on the United States, which quickly concluded the need to construct a plan that would enable European economic recovery. In June

1947, US Secretary of State General George Marshall outlined a plan to offer economic assistance to aid the recovery of all European states, declaring that 'Europe's requirements for the next three or four years of foreign food and other essential products – principally from America – are so much greater than her present ability to pay that she must have substantial additional help or face economic, social and political deterioration of a very grave character' [*Doc.4*]. The plan, which proved to be a tremendous success, aimed to promote intra-European trade and create a marketplace that was similar to the US. In aiming to speed up the process of European economic recovery, the United States hoped that an upturn in Europe's fortunes would lessen the dependence on American aid. To avoid criticism that the Marshall Plan was part of a broader US anti-communist policy (an argument that was levelled at the Truman Doctrine), the plan was open to a large number of countries [*Doc.4*]. But only Western European governments accepted the aid, an outcome that further cemented the division between America and the Soviet Union.

It is therefore evident that barely two years after the end of the Second World War there was a bipolar division of Europe based on Soviet and US spheres of influence. This situation would continue for a further four decades until the dramatic break-up of the Soviet-dominated Eastern bloc in 1989–90. The intervening cold war proved to be the defining feature of international politics and the institutions that emerged during this period – which in the case of Western Europe included the North Atlantic Treaty Organisation (NATO) and the EEC and in the case of Eastern Europe included the Warsaw Treaty Organisation (or Warsaw Pact) and the founding of the Comecon – served to demonstrate both the division of Europe along East–West lines and the role which the superpowers played in underpinning these institutions. It was accordingly the case that the combination of this division and the tension between the two superpowers proved to be both the defining feature of international politics and an instrumental factor in fostering the origins of European integration.

Superpower influence within the European arena was reflected in the rapid assertion of Soviet influence in Eastern Europe: by 1948 Czechoslovakia, East Germany and Poland were under Moscow's influence. In March 1948 the Soviet Union commenced a policy of restricting Western access to Berlin which materialised into a total blockade of land access to the city by June of that year. This 'Berlin crisis' would result in 1.6 million tons of clothing, food, fuel and other necessities being airlifted to the city until the Soviets lifted their blockade on 12 May 1949, and would be followed in 1961 by the erection of the Berlin Wall. The Berlin crisis helped to institutionalise the cold war and influenced the decision of Britain, France, Belgium, Luxembourg and the Netherlands to sign the Brussels Treaty in March 1948, committing the participating members to a system of collective self-defence

[*Doc.6*]. Just over one year later, in April 1949, the principle of collective self-defence would evolve into the signing of the North Atlantic Treaty in Washington by Belgium, Canada, Denmark, France, Iceland, Italy, Luxembourg, the Netherlands, Norway, Portugal, the United Kingdom and the United States. NATO was significant not just because of the commitment to collective self-defence, whereby if one member was attacked then all the other members would be obliged to respond, but because US involvement provided an important balance of power within Europe [*Doc.7*].

In addition to military and security developments, the division of Europe was highlighted by economic factors. The Organisation for European Economic Cooperation (OEEC) was established in April 1948 with the purpose of supervising the Marshall Aid programme which provided just over $12.5 billion in aid to Europe between 1948 and 1951. Based on an intergovernmental method of cooperation, the OEEC managed to lower trade barriers among European nations and provided the first small step towards European economic cooperation. But despite the success of the OEEC, many countries argued that it lacked the necessary supranational structures to bring long-term changes to the economic and political situation in Western Europe. This was a view shared by Schuman and Monnet. Monnet commented: 'I could not help seeing the intrinsic weakness of a system that went no further than mere cooperation between governments . . . The countries of Western Europe must turn their national efforts into a truly European effort. This will be possible only through a federation of the West' (Monnet, 1978: 272–3). To remedy this situation, 'a start would have to be made by doing something more practical and more ambitious. National sovereignty would have to be tackled more boldly and on a narrower front' (Monnet: 1978: 274). For Monnet, the successful integration of Europe could be achieved only by the creation of institutions.

Not all European nations were willing to accept the loss of sovereignty that supranational cooperation required. Britain, Portugal and many of the Scandinavian countries favoured intergovernmental cooperation that did not lessen the authority of their elected governments. The British position could partly be defended on economic grounds. It continued to be a relatively vibrant trading nation with many interests beyond the European theatre: its coal and steel production after 1945 far exceeded that of other European countries. A perception that Britain was a significant power led Churchill in the early 1950s to advance the concept of 'three great circles among the free nations and democracies' – that embraced the Commonwealth, the English-speaking world and Europe – and crucially, Britain played a key role in each of them. Churchill therefore argued that Britain's leadership of the Commonwealth, 'special relationship with the United States' and connection to Europe meant that Britain was 'the only country which has a great part in every one of them'.

Yet while it was perfectly true that Britain did have a role in each of these circles, it was not a permanent one. It is therefore hard to disagree with David Reynolds' view that 'In the decade from 1955 Britain's relationship with America became one of dependence, the Commonwealth and Sterling Area crumbled, and Western Europe was transformed by the creation of the EEC without British participation. Underlying all three developments was the country's rapid and catastrophic decline' (Reynolds, 2000: 190). Other European nations, by contrast, came to a far quicker understanding that their interests were best served through the creation of new institutional structures. The Benelux states, France and Italy had come to the conclusion that supranational cooperation offered a number of advantages which more than offset any loss of national sovereignty. Italy, for instance, considered that the new structures would offer it a degree of legitimacy in the international community which it needed because of its alliance with Germany during the Second World War.

THE HAGUE CONGRESS

Much of the impetus behind supranational beliefs was in fact a product of wartime resistance movements that directly led to the formation of the European Union of Federalists (UEF) in December 1946. In the early post-1945 period the dominant approach to European integration was federalism. The federalist approach envisaged the creation of a federal constitution for Europe whereby a federal parliament, government and court would be entrusted with certain powers over such policy areas as security and trade, with the remaining policies to be dealt with by the different levels of government within the member states. The crux of the plan was that the member states would be linked by certain common policies that would be governed by an institutional structure at a level above national governments. The desire of the federalists to create an appropriate constitution resulted in the decision to hold a conference of interested parties, eventually held in The Hague in May 1948.

The Hague Congress attracted 750 delegates from a range of nongovernmental organisations. Its Honorary President was Winston Churchill, who in 1946 had called for a 'United States of Europe' [*Doc.3*]. But while Churchill considered that France and Germany should form the key partnership in the reconstruction of Europe (a view shared by Monnet), his views did not extend to Britain taking a leading role in such a union. This mirrored the then Labour government's standpoint that favoured a policy of independence; relations with Europe were placed within the context of Britain's extensive network of trading linkages to the Commonwealth and America. Moreover, whereas France favoured the establishment of new structures to control Germany, this was less of a concern to policy-makers in London who tended to view European cooperation within the wider context of resisting Soviet influence [*Doc.5*]. But even in the realm of military affairs Britain had come to the conclusion that its security interests were best served by its relationship with America rather than with a war-beaten Western Europe. As a consequence Britain championed the 1949 North Atlantic Treaty Organisation (which crucially involved a US commitment) [*Doc.7*] and at the same time showed no interest in the discussions that took place at The Hague. Yet when these discussions led to the formation of the Council of Europe in May 1949 [*Doc.8*], Britain, despite its reservations, was one of the ten founder members.

The Council of Europe, which by 2004 had 45 members, met on an annual basis and provided the first opportunity for the rehabilitation of West Germany when it became a member in 1950. But while the Council of Europe aimed 'to achieve a greater unity between its Members', the fact that it sought to do this 'by discussion of questions of common concern and by agreements and common action in economic, social, cultural, scientific, legal and administrative matters and in the maintenance and further realisation of human rights and fundamental freedoms' meant that there was an extremely broad and vague remit for discussion [*Doc.8*]. As one commentator has noted: 'This was so vague as to be virtually meaningless: in practice there was nothing in the Council structure which facilitated action as distinct from talk' (Henig, 2002: 23). Moreover, in contrast to the wishes of the federalists who had provided the initiative behind the Hague meeting, the structure of the Council of Europe was based on intergovernmental rather than federal designs. As such it did not involve the transfer of power and influence away from nation states that was so desired by the federalist movement, whose members quickly realised its powerlessness. At the time, British ministers and officials could have come to the conclusion that its preference for intergovernmental structures had triumphed over federalist desires for the reconstruction of Europe. Such an assessment was boosted by two further factors. First, the establishment of strong postwar welfare policies in most European states lessened the demand for the European solutions that the federalists advocated. Second, the United States had reservations over solutions to European integration that sprang from resistance and/or communist initiatives and pressure.

THE COAL AND STEEL COMMUNITY

By the end of the 1940s it was increasingly clear that a strong Germany was central to the economic rehabilitation of Europe and vital in the emerging cold war conflict with the Soviet Union. The implication here was clear: if Germany was going to take on a greater role and become an 'equal' partner with other European states, the restrictions imposed on it at the end of the war would have to be removed. Britain and America were particularly supportive of the reintegration of Germany and of the need to lift the restrictions. France was less keen and had refused to merge its occupation zone in Germany with that of Britain and America (the latter two had merged to create the Bizone in December 1946). For obvious reasons, France had been keen to maintain its control over the coal resources of the Ruhr as a means of restricting the resurgence of German power and as a way of assisting with the modernisation of the French economy. Yet British and American pressure to lift restrictions on Germany, combined with British reluctance to take the lead in Europe, meant that by 1949 France was in search of a new policy that sought to permit German economic recovery and reconcile French security concerns about a resurgent Germany.

How was this to be accomplished? In the absence of British leadership, France took the lead in addressing the combined issues of Europe's need to contain Germany and Germany's need for equality. For these twin objectives of political integration and the normalisation of closer relations between France and Germany to occur Monnet proposed the creation of a supranational coal and steel community. Coal and steel were chosen because they were the most important economic industries at the time and had been influential in the friction that resulted in two world wars. Monnet lost no time in managing to persuade the French Foreign Minister, Robert Schuman, to adopt his proposals and these were made clear in the opening gambits of the Schuman Declaration of 9 May 1950: 'The French Government proposes that Franco-German coal and steel production should be placed under a common High Authority in an organisation open to the other countries of Europe' [*Doc.9*]. As Monnet himself commented: 'The Schuman proposals are revolutionary or they are nothing . . . The indispensable first principle of these proposals is the abnegation of sovereignty in a limited but decisive field . . . Any plan which does not involve this indispensable first principle can make no useful contribution to the solution of the grave problems that face us . . . What must be sought is a fusion of the interests of the European peoples . . .' (Monnet, 1978: 316). The significance of the declaration lay in the desire of France to forfeit an amount of national sovereignty through the creation of new supranational structures in an effort to create peace and as such it is generally regarded as the key action in the construction of Europe.

This 'functionalist' approach to integration was notably different from the federalist approach that had been behind the Hague Congress. The functionalist approach was based on the principle of a gradual transfer of sovereignty from nation states in specific policy areas that Monnet thought would be acceptable to the member states. Influenced by the work of David Mitrany, the functionalist approach was thus significantly less ambitious and far-reaching than the federalist viewpoint (Mitrany, 1946). The great hope of functionalists was that peace could be achieved through the furtherance of integration in specific sectors of the economy, such as agriculture or coal, with these sectors governed by supranational institutions. Although methods of decision-making would be determined by member states outside the specific sector of the economy, functionalists nonetheless considered that the success of integration in one sector would create 'spillover' pressures that would result in a demand for more integration in other areas (Haas, 1968: 283). Monnet's assumption was therefore that in an effort to capitalise on the benefits of integration, member states would agree to other policy areas being incorporated into the European fold. But although Monnet's approach was successful initially, the underlying assumption that European integration would proceed on a logical and rational path was not borne out by the events of later years.

Belgium, Italy, Luxembourg and the Netherlands responded positively to the Schuman Declaration, not least because it provided a useful mechanism to accelerate the process of industrial modernisation. Germany was particularly enthusiastic. 'It was a way of giving more freedom of manoeuvre to the German coal and steel industry; it allayed French anxiety over their security; and it had the full and enthusiastic support of the American government' (Paterson, 1994: 143). Britain, by contrast, while aware of the benefits offered by the Schuman Plan in forging closer Franco-German cooperation, felt no compulsion to get involved in a process that centred on the decisions of a new higher authority being binding on the participating member states. Matters were not helped by the fact that Schuman had deliberately not consulted Britain about the proposal as a result of his fear that London would thwart the initiative. Yet it is extremely unlikely that Britain would have responded in any other manner even if it had been specifically consulted. This was because the Schuman Declaration was not merely concerned with the coordination of coal and steel production. It stressed that 'the pooling of coal and steel production will immediately ensure the establishment of common bases for economic development as a first step in the federation of Europe, and will change the destinies of those regions which have long been devoted to the manufacture of arms, to which they themselves were the constant victims' [*Doc.9*].

Britain, which had been content with the intergovernmental structures of the OEEC, did not feel the need to re-establish itself in a new form of organisation. The diversity and 'relative' strength of Britain's trade – after 1945 it produced approximately two-thirds of the steel of what would become 'the Six' – meant that it did not consider its influence on world events would be enhanced by joining forces with other countries. Such a viewpoint contrasted the position of many of the governments of the six who, faced with a combination of domestic economic difficulties, the threat of Soviet communism and a decline in Europe's influence in the world economy, regarded participation in a new organisation to be the only means to overcome these challenges. It is a point that Alan Milward has made in arguing that European integration took place as a result of the demands of the nation states (Milward, 1992). Both Italy and Germany, for instance, considered European integration to be a central means by which they could re-establish themselves, while for other nations, such as France, it reduced their fear of a revived Germany.

Britain's policy of favouring loose association rather than integration with Europe was shaped by a refusal to accept Schuman's condition that all member states had to agree to the principle of supranational cooperation *prior* to engaging in the talks that were to work out the details of the Schuman Plan. As a result the British government rejected the Schuman Plan on the grounds that its supranationalism would impact on national sovereignty. Britain was therefore absent when 'the Six' states of Belgium, France, Germany, Italy, Luxembourg and the Netherlands met at the beginning of June 1950 to commence discussions on the Schuman Plan. Jean Monnet, who chaired the talks, stressed the importance of progressing beyond the national negotiating position: 'We are here,' he said, 'to undertake a common task – not to negotiate for our own national advantage, but to seek it in the advantage of all. Only if we eliminate from our debates any particular feelings shall we reach a solution. In so far as we, gathered here, can change our methods, the attitude of all Europeans will likewise change' (Monnet, 1978: 323).

The outcome of these negotiations was the formation of a European Coal and Steel Community Treaty that was designed to last for 50 years and whose founding treaty was signed in Paris by the representatives from Belgium, France, Germany, Italy, Luxembourg and the Netherlands on 18 April 1951; the process of ratification was completed by the end of June 1952 [*Doc.11*]. The underlying objective of the Treaty was to foster 'economic expansion, growth of employment and a rising standard of living' in the member states by means of creating a common market in coal and steel that would be managed by joint institutions on the basis of agreed policies. Such policies would embrace consumption, development, expansion, prices, production, trade and the economic and social conditions of employees working within the industry. One impact of these policies was the immediate abolition of all coal and steel import and export duties and the removal of all national subsidies for these commodities.

Despite the fact that the Treaty focused only on a specific sector of the economy, the preamble demonstrated the desire of the founding fathers to move beyond coal and steel to create a wider Community by means of functional integration and political spillover. 'The idea was to create a federal prototype. Once "a practical community of interests" had been created, mentalities would change, other steps would become possible, a new dynamic would begin to operate and finally, step by step, lead to a federal destination' (Duchêne, 1996: 55). Thus, at the heart of the ECSC lay a sector-by-sector approach to European integration. In this context, the founding member states 'resolved to substitute for age-old rivalries the merging of their essential interests; to create, by establishing an economic community, the basis for a broader and deeper community among peoples long divided by bloody conflicts; and to lay the foundations for institutions which will give direction to a destiny henceforward shared' [*Doc.11*]. This, combined with the supranational institutional structure of the ECSC, ensured that it was distinguishable from other efforts to promote European cooperation, such as the Council of Europe.

Monnet, who had chaired the talks, was elected the first President of the ECSC (1952–56). The four institutions that governed it included a High Authority (subsequently the European Commission), which Monnet argued should be independent of the member states. Moreover, as an executive institution Monnet stressed that it should take responsibility for the coal and steel industries of 'the Six' (members) and establish common policies on such issues as working conditions and prices. The Treaty also established a Council of Ministers, composed of one representative from each member state and which had to be consulted by the High Authority. A European Court of Justice was also created to resolve disputes among the member states and between them and the ECSC, and although a Common Assembly was created to inject a degree of democracy, the pattern of weak democratic control was established and this 'democratic deficit' would in later years become a particularly contentious issue.

In short, the significance of the ECSC lay in the capacity for European integration to progress beyond initiatives such as the Council of Europe, whose vague aims did little to unite European nations. The ECSC thus offered a new form of organisation where nation states agreed to surrender an element of their sovereignty to a supranational institution. Yet at the same time it had a limited membership and many OEEC members, such as Britain, were not part of the ECSC. Its structures also did not reflect the full federation for which many had campaigned. But despite this compromised outcome, it provided the first attempt to integrate the states of Europe in a structure that differed from the intergovernmental principles of the OEEC and NATO.

THE FAILURE OF THE EUROPEAN DEFENCE COMMUNITY

Just as the economic concerns of a postwar Germany provided the impetus behind the ECSC, the security concerns of a future remilitarised Germany were central to the development of the European Defence Community. In the climate of the cold war, the US was particularly keen to revive German military power and for the country to become a member of NATO as a means of countering the threat of the Soviet 'Red Army' in the European theatre. At the same time, the wider global tension between the US and the Soviet Union had been accentuated by the successful Soviet atomic test in the autumn of 1949 and the outbreak of the Korean War in 1950. A militarily revived Germany would nonetheless be a matter of concern for France, which initially opposed the American plans for German rearmament. Indeed, as a significant proportion of the French army had been involved in Indo-China since 1946, German rearmament would quickly result in it having the largest army in Western Europe. Once again Monnet found a solution to this problem when he advocated that the principle of supranational cooperation could be extended into the remit of defence. Monnet's idea was therefore to mimic the example of the Schuman Plan to promote the creation of a European defence system. In turn, the premier of France, René Pleven, suggested in October 1950 that France, Germany and other interested countries should establish a supranational European Army of 100,000 soldiers. Thus, just as supranationalism had been used to control German industry, so too would it be used to control German rearmament.

Such a proposal built on the Dunkirk Treaty of March 1947 and the Brussels Treaty of March 1948 [*Doc.6*]. (The latter had committed Britain, France and the Benelux nations to a common defence system at a time when the stability of Europe was threatened by the Soviet Union, most notably in the form of the Berlin blockade of 1948 and before NATO was founded.) Britain, which had been absent from the ECSC discussions, reacted negatively to the Pleven Plan with its proposal for a multinational force that would be responsible to a European Assembly and a European minister of defence. But for other countries, the Plan's attractions lay in the fact that it locked Germany into a defence system [*Doc.10*]. It was with this in mind that Belgium, France, Germany, Italy and Luxembourg commenced a process of negotiations in February 1951 that would eventually result in the signing of the European Defence Community Treaty in May 1952 [*Doc.12*]. The Netherlands, which was the remaining member of the 'six' ECSC nations, joined the EDC discussions in October 1951.

The outlook for European integration in 1952 initially appeared to be positive. But within a short time it became ever more gloomy and underscored the limitations of Monnet's approach to European integration. France was particularly keen to exercise its stamp on the shape of postwar Europe and did not view its relationship with Germany as that of an equal. Thus, while the EDC Treaty stressed that Germany should not have an independent military command, the other members were able to keep their own defence structures, albeit with the armed forces placed under a new supranational structure. This meant that all parties to the Treaty would have to forgo some degree of their capacity for independent action. This was something to which many politicians in France, particularly the Gaullists, were opposed as it implied the relinquishing of national command of the French army. Such nationalist arguments were influential behind the failure of the French National Assembly on 30 August 1954 to ratify the EDC Treaty. Indeed, it was only in the 1990s that member states were prepared to extend the EC's competence into defence matters.

The failure of the ambitious EDC plan – which would have led also to the creation of a European Political Community – was a notable setback for Monnet's approach to European integration and progress towards the building of supranational institutions. Nevertheless, the underlying issue of German remilitarisation remained an important topic on the European political landscape. To deal with this problem, the British Foreign Secretary (from 1955 Prime Minister), Anthony Eden, put forward a Foreign Office scheme which proposed that the 1948 Brussels Treaty (which had committed Britain, France and the Benelux states to a common defence system) should be expanded to include West Germany and Italy. For Britain, the key advantage of the proposal to create a new defence organisation – to be known as the Western European Union (WEU) – was that its intergovernmental structure meant that it did not contain the supranational features of the EDC, with the new policy being accepted by Belgium, France, Germany, Italy, Luxembourg, the Netherlands and Britain as a result of the modification of the Brussels Treaty by the Paris Agreements of 23 October 1954 [*Doc.13*]. In addition to this championing of the WEU, Eden argued that the crucial issue of German rearmament should take place within NATO, which Germany eventually joined in May 1955. And it would be this security dependence on the USA via NATO, rather than the WEU, which would act as the formal check on German armament.

The absence of supranational structures in the WEU represented a bitter blow to the federalist movement. The WEU differed little from the loose intergovernmental structure of the Brussels Treaty, with the only addition being a Consultative Assembly that would be attended by the same national delegates to the Common Assembly of the Council of Europe. From such a beginning the WEU never matured into a major security structure in the way that NATO did, but then again it was not meant to. It was clear from the outset that the WEU was not formed to duplicate the work of other organisations, while the military responsibility of the Council was handed over to NATO from the very beginning. In short, the collapse of the EDC and its replacement by the WEU demonstrated the decline of the attractiveness of the Community idea advanced by Monnet and Schuman.

This state of affairs, combined with the desire of France to strengthen the position of the member states within the ECSC, influenced Monnet's decision to announce his resignation as President of the ECSC in November 1954. Impatient for further advances in European integration, he had become disenchanted with the resistance of some member states. In a statement to the ECSC Common Assembly in Strasbourg, Monnet stressed that 'It is for Parliaments and Governments to decide on the transfer of new powers to the European institutions. The impulse must therefore come from without. [In resigning as President], I shall be able to join in the efforts of all those who are working to continue and enlarge what has begun' (Monnet, 1978: 400).

To do this, Monnet established a pressure group of like-minded Europeans known as the 'Action Committee for the United States of Europe', formed on 13 October 1955 with Monnet serving as President until his resignation on 9 May 1975.

Monnet's departure from the ECSC proved to be a significant shock to the national governments and raised the key question of what would now happen. The response was to come from the Benelux governments. In a memorandum that was drafted on their behalf by the Belgian Foreign Minister, Paul-Henri Spaak, they advocated the taking of further steps towards integration by establishing a common market and creating an atomic energy community. This in turn formed part of the discussions that took place at a meeting in Messina in June 1955.

THE TREATIES OF ROME

In June 1955 the foreign ministers of the Six met in Messina (Italy) to discuss proposals for further European integration, of which the fields of transport and atomic energy were considered to be two possible options. As France was the only country to possess a nuclear energy programme, it had been the main champion of Euratom, a policy which it hoped to dominate within the Community. Moreover, as the costs associated with the policy were considered to be too great for just one country, France hoped to benefit from the greater levels of funding available from the Community. In essence, French support for European integration was shaped by its desire to secure its national interests. The end product was a resolution that noted that 'The Governments of the Federal Republic of Germany, Belgium, France, Italy, Luxembourg and the Netherlands believe the time has come to make a fresh advance towards the building of Europe. They are of the opinion that this must be achieved, first of all, in the economic field' [*Doc.14*].

To take the Messina Resolution forward, a committee was formed that included relevant experts and government representatives, chaired by the Belgian foreign minister Paul-Henri Spaak. Other leading figures in the discussions included Monnet and the Dutch foreign minister Johan Beyen. Beyen's contributions proved to be particularly crucial, as he argued for the creation of a customs union and common market that reduced trade barriers between the Six. This approach differed from the widely held viewpoint that integration should proceed on sectoral grounds alone and Beyen's plans were therefore more ambitious.

Not all states shared Beyen's view of European integration. Britain was particularly hostile to the creation of a common market as the government believed plans to create a customs union represented a form of protectionism that did not mirror Britain's preference for open and multilateral trading relationships. Such economic concerns masked a far more important reason for Britain's refusal to participate in the EEC: a rejection of the supranational powers of the Community's institutions. Britain's preferences were framed within the context of 'cooperation without commitment' and government ministers hoped to be able to steer the outcome in a non-supranational direction. Yet it was a highly unrealistic objective as the Spaak Committee's thoughts clearly involved the principle of some loss of national sovereignty. The longer Britain continued to take part in the discussions, the harder it would be for the British government to distance itself from being committed to the result. Britain therefore withdrew from the discussions in November 1955 when the government concluded that its proposal to establish a free trade area was not acceptable to the Six. Spaak would later comment that 'little by little the British attitude changed from one of mildly disdainful scepticism to growing fear' (Spaak, 1971: 232). Where did this leave Britain?

As an alternative, the British government pushed for intergovernmental cooperation within the OEEC. It was an approach that nevertheless proved unacceptable to the other member states (which Britain had wrongly thought would be unwilling to accept the objective of a common market) because they wanted a supranational rather than intergovernmental solution. And although Britain further clarified its position by drawing up a proposal for an alternative free trade association in November 1956, the Spaak Committee had already recommended in its April 1956 report that a common market and atomic energy community should be created. Such a conclusion was the product of the argument put forward by the Spaak Committee that further sectoral integration on the model of the ECSC would not work. As such, the Committee's report took the extremely significant step of abandoning further sectoral integration and instead advocated the creation of an Atomic Energy Community and a separate customs union. The Spaak Committee's report in turn formed the basis of the subsequent intergovernmental negotiations of the Six that commenced in June 1956 and ended in February 1957. The negotiations, which were often of a difficult nature, produced common agreements that resulted in the creation of the EEC and Euratom. The agreements were signed in Rome by the six member states of the ECSC on 25 March 1957 [*Doc.15*]. Both treaties were swiftly ratified by the national parliaments and came into effect on 1 January 1958 and in so doing marked a key moment in the history of Europe.

CHAPTER THREE

CONSTRUCTING THE COMMUNITY: 1958–68

INSTITUTIONAL DESIGN

Nearly 13 years after the end of the Second World War, the European Economic Community and European Atomic Energy Community took effect on 1 January 1958. Combined with the ECSC they formed the core of the European Communities. The Treaties of Rome provided the EEC with four main institutions: a Commission, a Council of Ministers, a Court of Justice and an Assembly (the latter two were shared with the ECSC and Euratom). An Economic and Social Committee was additionally created to act as a consultative body for the Council and Commission. The different institutional apparatus of the three institutions would continue to exist until June 1967 when they were merged to create a single Council of Ministers and a single Commission for the three European Communities [*Doc.19*].

The main supranational aspect of the EEC and its central administrative body consisted of a Commission (replacing the ECSC High Authority) whose primary task was to ensure that the provisions of the Treaty and the policies that flowed from it were properly administered, and to initiate and recommend policies to the Council of Ministers. This was a responsibility that the Commission more than adequately performed in the early years under the leadership of its first President, Walter Hallstein (who had been Monnet's main collaborator in the negotiation of the ECSC Treaty). The Commissioners (who headed individual departments) were, despite their appointment by member states, not representatives of the member states. Each Commissioner took an oath of loyalty to the EEC and swore 'neither to seek nor to take instructions from any government or body'. Federalists hoped that the Commission would act as the driving force behind European integration and that it would not be constrained by the politicking of member states. This was a position that was not shared by de Gaulle who did not accept the federalist vision and who, on his return to power in June 1958, would argue against the enhancement of the Commission's powers.

Although the Commission contained an explicit supranational design, it was not the only institution that had a supranational focus. Observers could be forgiven for assuming that as the national interests of member states were reflected in the Council of Ministers (the second major EEC institution), the Council was devoid of supranationalism. To be sure, the Council's composition of national government ministers – with varied membership depending on the agenda – reflected an intergovernmental design that was further confirmed by the fact that each member state took its turn in chairing the meetings (a duty that rotated every six months). However, as the Treaty of Rome included a provision for decisions to be taken on a qualified majority basis from 1966 (as opposed to just a unanimity basis), it would be possible for a nation's interests to be overridden by the views of the majority. And in so far as majority and qualified majority voting were viewed to be of importance in ensuring that the Community's progress could not be hijacked by the views of any one member state, it was a process that contained an element of supranationalism. Moreover, it would provide the pretext for the French President, Charles de Gaulle, to block the Community's proceedings in the second half of 1965 [*Doc.20*]. Curiously, there were few concerns about this process in the early days of the Community's existence.

To assist member states with the administrative tasks of the Council meetings, a Committee of Permanent Representatives (Coreper) was created in 1958, although it would not be until the Merger Treaty of 1967 that it would obtain the status of a full legal institution of the Community [*Doc.19*]. The national representatives that made up this body were to play an important role in the functioning of the Community, having the responsibility to provide preparatory briefings to government ministers and to take uncontroversial decisions. Yet, while this body served to bolster the interests of the member states, it was the decision taken by the leaders of national governments to meet at summits that cemented the position of member states, the first meeting taking place in Paris in February 1961.

The third major institution created by the Treaty of Rome was the Parliamentary Assembly which served as a direct replacement for the advisory body that was provided for by the ECSC Treaty. The Parliamentary Assembly – which in 1962 was renamed the European Parliament – was provided with a limited number of supervisory powers over the Commission and the Council of Ministers. This included the right to put questions to the Commission, to discharge the annual budget and to censure the Commission (a power that was not used until 1999). The powers entrusted to the European Parliament were for the most part of a limited nature and this meant that it exercised little effective control over the European Commission or the Council of Ministers. Individual Commissioners could not be sacked by the Parliament and this institution had little influence over budgetary matters and no ability to force amendments to legislation. This state of affairs continued for the next three decades, with the European Parliament's institutional weakness finally addressed in the 1993 Treaty on European Union when it obtained a more decisive role in the decision-making process (co-decision procedure).

To ensure that the laws of the Community were implemented in a common format, a Court of Justice was established as the fourth major institution. Based in Luxembourg, the Court consisted of judges appointed upon the recommendation of member states for six-year renewable terms. The Court was given the specific responsibility of handling cases from all three Community treaties and from disputes arising between member states, member states and the Communities, individuals and member states and finally individuals and the Communities. Its decisions were taken by majority voting and were final. The very presence of Community law provided an important distinction between the Community and other international organisations, although it was nevertheless the case that Community law existed alongside national legal systems. So while the Treaty of Rome paid attention to developing supranational structures, a significant degree of influence was retained by the member states through intergovernmental structures. Just as the supranational Commission was entrusted with the responsibility for both initiating and implementing policies, the interests of the member states were reflected in the Council of Ministers which had the primary task of legislating on the basis of the proposals arising from the Commission. Of the remaining institutions, the Parliamentary Assembly's influence was of a limited nature, while the Court of Justice played a more significant role by interpreting EEC decisions. And although this balance between the supranational and intergovernmental would initially tilt in favour of the Commission, as the Community progressed into the second half of the 1960s the institutional battle would favour the member states.

POLICIES AND COMPETENCIES

A central aim of the new organisation was the creation of a customs union and common market to promote free and equal competition between the participating member states, being influenced by two main factors: first, a desire to create higher levels of economic growth; second, an aspiration that member states should not return to a system of national protectionism that had been a dominant feature before the war. Article 2 of the Treaty of Rome stressed that 'The Community shall have as its aim, by establishing a common market and progressively approximating the economic policies of member states, to promote throughout the Community a harmonious development of economic activities, a continuous and balanced expansion, an increase in stability, an accelerated raising of the standard of living and closer relations between its member states' [*Doc.15*].

The very creation of such a customs union resulted in the member states having to agree to certain common practices and standards that centred on eliminating the distinctions – and borders – between the different national markets. This included the abolition of tariffs and restrictive practices, such as price fixing and the dumping of products. In addition to these internal policies, member states agreed to the creation of a common external tariff to ensure that non-Community countries were presented with a common tariff irrespective of which member state they traded with. In the end, a full customs union was established by 1 July 1968, 18 months ahead of the schedule that had been laid down in the Treaty. But apart from these economic benefits, the federalists also hoped that over a period of time there would take place a gradual shift of decision-making away from member states towards the European institutions. In other words, economic integration would lead to European unity within a wide variety of areas, including social affairs, financial matters and foreign policy.

Of these various areas, economic objectives proved to be the most easily attainable and by the end of the 1960s many of the objectives that had been set in this policy area had been met. The attainment of these objectives was greatly influenced by Walter Hallstein's dynamic leadership of the European Commission. In the period between 1958 and 1970, trade among the Six increased by five times, exports to the rest of the world increased by two-and-a-half times, and the gross domestic product (GDP) of Community member states grew at an annual average of 5 per cent. By 1962 the EEC was the world's largest single trading power. A combination of economic growth, the creation of united policies based on supranational institutions and the overall size of the combined economies of the Six increased the Community's influence on world affairs. This was evidenced by a desire to improve the access that the Six's former colonies had to the Community: in 1963 the Yaoundé Convention was signed between the Community and 18 African states and Madagascar, which would be further extended in 1969 with a second Yaoundé Convention. An awareness of the EEC's important role as a trading organisation led the Community to tackle the issue of market access with other developed countries, as highlighted by the 1967 Kennedy tariff rounds. As a demonstration of the external role being carved out by the EEC, and the recognition attached to it by the outside world, these negotiations reduced tariff barriers between Europe and North America and acted as a further stimulus to economic growth.

Despite these significant economic achievements, by the end of the 1960s the Community had not realised all of its initial objectives. The continuing presence of restrictions on the free movement of capital, goods and people ensured that the commitment in Article 3 of the Treaty of Rome to 'the abolition, as between member states, of obstacles to freedom of movement for persons, services and capital' and ergo the promotion of free and equal competition had not been achieved by 1970 [*Doc.15*]. The reason for this lack of progress can be attributed partly to the greater desire among policy-makers to eliminate tariff and quota barriers in the early stages of European integration rather than to tackle those policies that would aid the creation of a single market. Indeed, it would not be until the mid-1980s that plans would be set in motion that resulted in genuine free movement within the Community. Second, although a Social Fund had been created in the Treaty of Rome to assist with tackling unemployment, it was relatively small and it proved difficult to achieve common social, regional and transport policies. A key area where the Six did manage to achieve a common policy was the common agricultural policy (CAP). And although the policy was a direct response to the food shortage that existed in postwar Europe, it also represented a classic Community compromise. In return for dismantling the protective trading barriers that protected the French economy from foreign competition, the government in Paris argued for the creation of an agricultural policy to protect its farming interests (in excess of 20 per cent of the French workforce was employed in the agricultural sector of the economy at the time). As such, an important factor in the emergence of the CAP was its ability to satisfy French and German interests.

But while a common agricultural policy was referred to in the Treaty of Rome, it was not exactly clear how such a policy would operate in practice. The only guidance provided was that its aims were to secure the supply of agricultural produce by means of increasing production, stabilising prices and providing farmers with an adequate standard of living. In other words, a particular concern was the absence of concrete information as to how the CAP would be financed and this would, in a short period of time, provide the Community with a crucial crisis. Nonetheless, the CAP proved to be an important development for the Community for both economic and political reasons: in 1955 it accounted for a significant percentage of the share of the labour force and made a notable contribution to national GDP. The respective figures were: France 25.9 per cent of the labour force and 12.3 per cent of GDP, Italy 39.5 per cent and 21.6 per cent, Germany 18.9 per cent and 8.5 per cent, Luxembourg 25 per cent and 9 per cent, the Netherlands 13.7 per cent and 12 per cent, and Belgium 9.3 per cent and 8.1 per cent (Hix, 1999: 255). Co-operation on agricultural policy also demonstrated the willingness of the member states to establish a common policy that Hallstein considered to be 'vital to the future of the Community' (Hallstein, 1962: 54). In practical terms it would necessitate bringing together distinct national systems of agricultural support, the work of which would be taken over by supranational organisations. The first regulations on agricultural matters were introduced in January 1962 and by 1968 a fully effective agricultural policy was in existence. To achieve its goal of plentiful production, the CAP established a rather complex system that provided farmers with subsidies and price guarantees, being administered by a European Agricultural Guidance and Guarantee Fund. (The guidance element focused on matters relating to agricultural structural reform while matters relating to the price mechanism were dealt with by the guarantee element of the fund.)

Yet while there is much truth in the assessment that the CAP was a success story because of its efforts in forging closer integration, the CAP has nonetheless been subject to a significant amount of criticism. This has been not least as a result of the sums of money involved. To encourage agricultural production, the CAP provided farmers with a guaranteed price for their products which essentially meant that producers inside the Community were more favourably placed than overseas competitors. Moreover, so as to place its own market at an advantage, the Community established a system of tariffs and customs duties that protected farmers from lower-cost imports. Such a system encouraged efficient farmers to maximise output and consequently led to significant variance in the level of support provided, whereby large farms benefited over small farms. Apart from putting a question mark over the 'common' nature of the CAP, the structural design of the system encouraged the production of surpluses that the Commission purchased to protect prices and guarantee farm income. This inevitably led to the creation of the so-called 'wine lakes' and 'butter mountains'.

Over-production and a policy of maintaining prices that were often higher than world market levels resulted in the CAP being subjected to intense criticism from within and outside the Community. This included the environmental impact of large-scale industrialised farming that encouraged the use of fertilisers. It was also an extremely expensive policy. The CAP accounted for approximately 50 per cent of the Community budget by the 1990s, and despite a number of attempts at reform it continues to account for in excess of 40 per cent of the budget in 2004. This is because the entrenched interests of the farming community that the CAP favoured (particularly within France) meant that it proved to be a difficult policy to reform and impossible to remove from the Community agenda. This is despite the fact that in contrast to its dominant position in the postwar economy, agriculture no longer accounts for a significant percentage of the national labour force or makes a major contribution to the GDP of member states. Between 1955 and 1995, 'the share of agriculture as a percentage of the labour force of the member states declined from over 20 per cent to under 10 per cent, and as a percentage of national income of the member states it declined from over 10 per cent to under 3 per cent' (Hix, 1999: 254–5).

THE NATIONALIST BACKLASH

Having decided not to take part in the negotiations that led to the EEC, the British government was determined to take the initiative and advance its own ideas for a free trade area that had no supranational elements. The 1956 Suez crisis – in which Britain was forced to withdraw from Egypt as a result of American economic and political pressure – had demonstrated that Britain was no longer a world power. Yet while the government advanced the case for a free trade area, it did not make the more logical deduction that British influence could be maximised through membership of the European Community. Simply put, the British proposal would involve the Six EEC countries being linked by association to the other OEEC countries in the form of a free trade area. Although aimed at uniting Europe, Britain hoped to have the best of both worlds: to maintain preferential trade arrangements with the Commonwealth and the colonies and at the same time to be linked to the Community. But despite these rather selfish aims, the basic concept of a free trade area received warm support in many of the capitals of the Six. Germany and Italy were broadly in favour, although France was more sceptical and there were notable differences between its views and those of Britain. The British government advocated a free trade area based on a loose set of rules, the maintenance of Commonwealth preferences, a rejection of the need to harmonise a range of policies from tariffs to trade policies, and an unwilling-ness to include agriculture. The French negotiators adopted a totally con-trary stance in all of these matters. All in all, the discussions proved fruitless. The British proposal – which lacked any supranational content – was unattractive to the Six (particularly France) which had acknowledged the need for supranationalism in their acceptance of the Treaty of Rome. More importantly, it is evident that if Britain's free trade idea had been successful, it would have transformed the EEC into a large free trade area that would have had a damaging impact on the process of integration that the Six desired.

By 1958 the process of integration had, in any case, started with the first tariff cuts among EEC countries. And having commenced this course of action, the Six were unwilling to allow members of a free trade area to obtain the benefits of access to EEC markets without accepting the responsibilities of the customs union. Willis reports that the then French Information Minister Jacques Soustelle commented in November 1958 that 'it was clear to France that it was not possible to create the free trade area in the way the British wanted' (Willis, 1968: 280). This remark signalled the death of the negotia-tions which formally came to an end in December 1958 and which in turn resulted in seven of the remaining eleven members of the OEEC commencing a process of discussions that would eventually lead to the creation of the European Free Trade Association (EFTA). The seven non-EEC countries of Austria, Britain, Denmark, Norway, Portugal, Sweden and Switzerland accordingly signed the Stockholm Convention on 4 January 1960, thereby marking the creation of EFTA. It was purely concerned with the achievement of a free trade area – based on intergovernmental cooperation – and contained none of the economic or political integration that its members had found so unwelcome in the Treaty of Rome.

The British government's decision to champion open trading relations through EFTA had been based on a belief that its economic, political and security interests were noticeably different from those held by other European nations. British policy-makers considered that the majority of Britain's trade would continue to focus on the Commonwealth, in particular the English-speaking countries of Australia, Canada and New Zealand. It was a viewpoint that was carved out of Britain's historical past and did not fully reflect the postwar reality of the declining importance of Commonwealth trade and the weakening of its overall influence on world affairs. Yet in a short period of time the British government reversed this stance and concluded that the looser ties of EFTA were of marginal benefit. Faced with a decline in its economic fortunes and global influence, the Conservative government of Harold Macmillan announced in July 1961 that Britain would make an application to join the EEC [*Doc.16*]. According to Edward Heath (who managed the 1961 application), '[T]he decision of Harold Macmillan's government to apply for membership of the European Community represented an historic moment in post-war politics. It determined the direction not just of British policy, but also that of Europe and the Atlantic alliance . . . It signalled the end of a glorious era, that of the British Empire, and the beginning of a whole new chapter of British history' (Heath, 1998: 203; *Doc.16*).

This change of strategy was based on economic, political and security grounds. As already mentioned, the 1956 Suez crisis highlighted the limitations of British military and political influence. Economic factors were also of considerable importance in influencing the government's decision to seek membership of the Community. Not only was Britain's economic growth flagging behind the Six (who were enjoying the benefits of economic integration and reductions in tariff barriers), but British trade with the countries of Western Europe was increasing at a faster rate than with the Empire and the Commonwealth. Finally, this reorientation of policy towards Europe reflected the preferences of the US, which was a strong advocate of Britain's entry and had been unsupportive of British plans for a free trade area. US support was influenced by a consideration that Britain's membership would help to defend American interests and dilute the Franco–German relationship. Macmillan thus concluded that it would be better to maintain Britain's 'special relationship' with the US inside rather than outside the EEC.

Despite the economic and political arguments for membership, the application was framed within the wider context of continued links to the Commonwealth and the US. Such a position did not find favour from France, who under De Gaulle's leadership was overtly hostile to American influence on NATO via European matters. And as Article 237 of the Treaty of Rome required that the admission of new member states to the Community was dependent on a unanimous vote within the Council of Ministers, Britain's application for membership could be torpedoed by a veto. In the end, this was the policy that de Gaulle used on the grounds that Britain's membership would destabilise the Community. In any event, the negotiations over the membership applications became linked to a wider debate about the future of the Community, as the economic progress that it had achieved led the Six to pay closer attention to matters of a political nature. Yet while most member states thought that the Community should play a greater role in world affairs, some countries, such as France, were of the opinion that this should not be at the expense of national influence. Although de Gaulle wanted a stronger Europe (partly to act as a counter to the influence of the US) and was also aware of the economic benefits that France obtained from membership, he questioned the need for the transfer of too many powers to the supranational institutions of the Community. To resolve this impasse, the leaders of the Six agreed at the 1961 Bonn summit to establish an intergovernmental committee, chaired by the French Ambassador Christian Fouchet, to examine the case for closer political integration. By the end of the year the Fouchet committee had produced a draft treaty that proposed the creation of an intergovernmental organisation outside of the Treaty of Rome to coordinate foreign and defence policy, and in doing so rejected the federal model.

For de Gaulle, a key aspect of the plan was that France's interests would be protected because decisions would be subject to unanimous agreement. Such a strategy reflected France's and de Gaulle's desire to rein back some of the powers which had been granted in the Treaty of Rome. The other members of the Community – particularly Belgium and the Netherlands – did not share this view and argued that the proposals would undermine the supranational design of the existing Community institutions through the separation of economic affairs from those of defence and security. As a consequence it proved impossible to reconcile the gulf between the desire of the majority to maintain the 'Community method' and de Gaulle's vision of 'l'Europe des Patries' (a Europe of nation states). An inability to resolve these differences of opinion resulted in the ending of discussions of the Fouchet Plan, which in turn led France to develop a bilateral foreign policy agreement with Germany, as set out in the January 1963 Franco–German Treaty of friendship [*Doc.18*]. The significance of the Franco–German Treaty – which provided for institutional cooperation between both countries across a broad range of policy areas – lay in the fact that it was the first bilateral relationship in the Community and in this context brought classical 'realpolitik' diplomacy among the Six. The Franco–German Treaty thus further cemented the role of member states as the key determinants about the future of European integration.

Even though the Fouchet Plan negotiations were not directly linked to Britain's application, the failure of the talks strengthened de Gaulle's uncertainties about the suitability of Britain joining an organisation that he wanted France to control. Thus, when Britain agreed to purchase the Polaris nuclear missile system from the US in December 1962, it provided de Gaulle with the necessary justification to veto Britain's membership application on the basis that Britain would be an American 'Trojan horse' in Europe [*Doc.17*]. Such was France's concern about American influence over European policy that de Gaulle subsequently withdrew France from the military command structure of NATO in 1966, which in turn brought about the need for NATO headquarters to relocate from Paris to Brussels.

De Gaulle's use of the veto ended any immediate hopes of Britain joining the Community. However, it did not necessarily signal a reorientation of British policy away from Europe. Writing in his diary after the veto, Harold Macmillan noted that 'the great question remains, "What is the alternative?" to the European Community. If we are honest, we must say there is none' (Macmillan, 1973: 374). Many of the other member states had welcomed the prospect of British membership as a means of counterbalancing French influence. Thus, not only did the veto sour relations between London and Paris but also between Paris and the capitals of the five other member states. This tension between de Gaulle's vision of European integration and that of the other member states came to a head in 1965 when the President of the European Commission, Walter Hallstein, put forward a package deal that combined measures to provide a financial basis for CAP with a requirement that the budgetary expenditure should be subject to parliamentary control (a policy advocated by the Netherlands). Hallstein considered these proposals to be necessary because the existing method of financing the relatively small Community budget out of national contributions would be inadequate for the considerable additional resources that the CAP necessitated. De Gaulle reacted to the proposals with considerable hostility as he favoured European integration based on free trade and an absence of supranationalism. He disliked the prospect of adding to the supranational power and independence of the Commission by providing the Community with its own resources from customs duties and agriculture levies, and saw no reason to support the Commission's proposals to augment the European Parliament's influence. But while de Gaulle was prepared to stand firm against the Commission's proposals, a far graver concern for him was the Treaty of Rome's provision to move from unanimity to majority voting in certain areas of the Council of Ministers' work from 1966 onwards. This change in voting procedure represented a strengthening of the supranational design of the Community and would in turn result in a reduction of national control.

An inability to resolve differences of opinion over the Commission's proposals led de Gaulle to prohibit his ministers from attending Council meetings from July to December 1965, a period commonly known as the 'empty chair crisis'. The crisis was finally resolved in January 1966, with the Hallstein Plan being abandoned in favour of the 'Luxembourg Compromise': member states agreed to an interim financial regulation for CAP, to limit the powers of the Commission and the European Parliament, and to introduce the procedure of majority voting with the provision that 'where very important interests are at stake the discussion must be continued until unanimous agreement is reached' [Doc.20]. In other words, a member state would be able to use a veto on those policies that it regarded to be at odds with its national interest. It was an outcome which indicated that member states would in future play an increasingly important role that would extend into the area of policy initiation. The Luxembourg Compromise thus signalled an important shift in power away from the Commission towards the national governments of the member states. Until 1965, the responsibility for initiating policy had rested principally with the Commission, which under the leadership of Walter Hallstein had successfully managed to forge ahead with the process of European integration. In the wake of the crisis, the Commission's role of formulating and initiating policy altered to that of a consensus builder that implemented agreements that were acceptable to the member states. And while this state of affairs served the immediate interests of many of the governments, it is widely accepted that the empty chair crisis and the Luxembourg Compromise limited the opportunity for further European integration over the next two decades. In this sense, as a result of the crisis, the Community's future development assumed the structure that it would maintain for the next 20 years. Indeed, it would not be until the 1987 Single European Act that the Community would engage in a process of reform that significantly went beyond the Luxembourg Compromise.

On 1 July 1967 the ECSC, Euratom and the EEC merged so that the three Communities – which remained intact – were served by a single Commission and Council of Ministers [Doc.19]. In practical terms, this referred to the coming together of the *executive* bodies as the three Communities already shared the Assembly (from 1962 the European Parliament) and the Court of Justice. Thus, the two Commissions of the EEC and Euratom, and the ECSC High Authority, merged into a single Commission of the European Communities. In addition to these changes, the Merger Treaty gave legal recognition to the Committee of Permanent Representatives (Coreper) which despite its absence of reference in the Treaty of Rome nonetheless proved to be a vital body in preparing the groundwork for ministerial meetings in the Council of Ministers. Apart from these institutional developments, a full customs union and the completion of CAP were also achieved.

The attainment of these objectives, combined with the Community's post-1965 attachment to intergovernmental methods of decision-making, ensured that the prospect of joining the EEC became increasingly attractive to a number of European countries. The question of enlargement reappeared in 1967 when the British Labour government, under the leadership of Harold Wilson, put forward a second application to join the Community [Doc.21]. Once again, the United States was supportive of this policy, hoping that

Britain's entry would strengthen the Atlantic link. But, as he had done before, de Gaulle vetoed the British application, pointing to the weakness of the British economy and the fact that London did not fully accept the constraints that membership of the Community implied. Observers might have thought that the British government would have withdrawn its application, as it had done in 1963. But this did not happen and the British application was instead 'left on the table' so that it could be reactivated at an appropriate time. In practical terms, this basically meant that Britain's prospects for membership would change only when de Gaulle was no longer in office. This would happen in 1969 when de Gaulle was forced to resign, less than a year after the May 1968 trade union and student unrest in France, and was succeeded by George Pompidou in April of that year.

By this stage French dominance over the Community could no longer be taken for granted: its economy was declining at a time when Germany was economically resurgent. A combination of concern over Germany's growing economic power and increased political assertiveness, as represented by the policy of *Ostpolitik* (rapprochement towards the Soviet bloc) carved out by its new Chancellor Willy Brandt, proved to be of great influence on French policy. Whereas de Gaulle had opposed the enlargement of the Community, Pompidou realised the potential value of British membership, which combined with France could act as a counterbalance to German influence. Under Pompidou, France began a process of constructing a more positive European policy that was once again shaped by a desire to control Germany.

Having overcome internal divisions, the Community entered the 1970s with its future appearing increasingly bright as it advanced towards a new phase of development. But despite the initial achievements of the early 1970s, the Community's progress for much of the decade was disrupted by a number of political and economic crises.

CHAPTER FOUR

FROM OPTIMISM TO INDECISION: 1969–79

THE SPIRIT OF THE HAGUE

A combination of concerns over Germany and domestic pressures for a positive French initiative towards the Community led French President Georges Pompidou to call a special meeting of the leaders of the six member states to be held at the Hague in December 1969 in order to 'relaunch' the Community [*Doc.22*]. In calling the Hague summit, Pompidou argued for the strengthening of existing Community competencies, the completion of the financing regimes for the common agricultural policy and the deepening of Community competencies in certain areas. Pompidou's desire to involve directly the leaders of the national governments was a deliberate attempt to inject some impetus into the Community, which had not experienced the automatic process of integration that the federalists had wished for. With de Gaulle no longer in office, the Hague summit of government leaders and foreign ministers provided an important opportunity to resolve a number of issues, which resulted, according to the Commission, in a 'turning point in its history' and led to 'the spirit of the Hague'. Agreement was reached on the question of enlargement (France had blocked Britain's applications in 1963 and 1967). A reversal of this policy under Pompidou was shaped by a hope that British accession would act as a balance to a resurgent Germany and limit the opportunity for the supranational development of the Community. But while Pompidou accepted the principle of enlargement, he refused to set a date for the accession negotiations to commence. He argued that enlargement could take place only once the question of the financing of the CAP – which had dogged the Community since 1965 – had been resolved. To resolve this impasse the other five members of the Community agreed to work out the question of CAP funding in return for France's guaranteed commitment to the commencement of enlargement negotiations.

In getting to the bottom of CAP funding, member states agreed in April 1970 to provide the Community with its own financial resources, a decision that represented a move away from direct national contributions. These 'own resources' extended beyond the remit of financing the CAP and were designed to ensure the Community had sufficient income to satisfy all the policies that the Commission administered. This funding would be achieved through a combination of agricultural levies charged on the importation of agricultural products from third countries, customs duties levied on industrial products imported into the Community, and a small amount of funding that would not exceed 1 per cent of the revenues a member state obtained from value added tax. In providing the Community with this financial base, member states divorced themselves from the process of inspecting expenditure. To remedy this 'accounting deficit', it was agreed to provide the European Parliament with the authority to examine the Community's budget (as the 1965 Hallstein Report had wanted). The implication of these developments was perfectly clear: it enhanced the supranational design of the Community.

What this funding agreement meant in practice was that those countries, such as Germany, that imported large quantities of agricultural produce and industrial goods would account for a greater proportion of the contributions to the Community's budget than a country that had fewer imports. But while the resolution of CAP funding paved the way for the future enlargement of the Community, the agreement was devoid of any input from those countries that wished to join the Community. It proved to be a crucial mistake. As a large industrialised economy with a small but efficient agricultural industry, Britain imported a substantial amount of foodstuffs. The 1970 agreement thus meant that Britain faced a requirement on its accession to the Community of having to pay significant sums into the Community budget at a time when its economic fortunes were in decline (which was a key reason for joining). Whereas the British government had hoped it would receive additional financial resources from the Community, it was instead faced with the horrifying prospect of providing a significant amount of its resources. Moreover, as Britain had a large industrial base and the smallest agricultural sector in the Community, it would receive little back in the way of CAP funding. Yet the overriding necessity of securing membership meant that it was a predicament the government was prepared to accept. All in all, this meant that Britain would become a net contributor to the EC and this disparity between Britain's low rate of economic growth and high budgetary contributions laid the groundwork for the subsequent budgetary disagreements that dominated the work of the Community in the late 1970s and early 1980s [*Doc.30*].

In addition to resolving the CAP funding, the Hague meeting was significant for its agreement to widen the Community's membership (paving the way for subsequent applications from Britain, Denmark, Ireland and Norway) and to deepen the EC's activities with a view to extending cooperation within the economic and political fields. To some observers, the simultaneous objectives of widening and deepening were incompatible: in an enlarged Community there would be less likelihood of achieving agreement on deeper European integration. Two committees were nonetheless established to examine the case for deeper economic and political integration. The premier of Luxembourg, Pierre Werner, was given the responsibility of leading a committee to examine the case for monetary union, while the Belgian diplomat (and future European Commissioner) Étienne Davignon led the committee which investigated the possibility of achieving closer political integration. The reports of both committees were published in 1970. The October Werner Report stressed that 'economic and monetary union is an objective realisable in the course of the present decade' (that is, by 1980) and that this would mean 'that the principal decisions of economic policy will be taken at Community level and therefore that the necessary powers will be transferred from the national plane to the Community plane' [*Doc.23*]. The significance of this declaration was nonetheless cautioned by the Werner Report emphasising that progress depended on 'the political will of the member states to realise this objective' [*Doc.23*]. Thus, while the Werner Report provided a blueprint for monetary union that could be attained in stages by 1980 and provided the motivation for member states to create a mechanism for managing and coordinating the different national currencies (the 1971 European currency management system, or 'the Snake'), the success of these objectives clearly rested on the support of the member states [*Doc.25*].

Having been instructed by the Hague summit 'to study the best way of achieving progress in the matter of political unification, within the context of enlargement' of the EC, the November 1970 Davignon Report recommended that foreign policy coordination 'should be the object of the first practical endeavours to demonstrate to all that Europe has a political vocation' [*Doc.24*]. In focusing on foreign policy, the Davignon Report pointed to the need for the EC to develop a stronger European voice in international affairs at a time when there was a notable gulf between the views of the United States and Western Europe on a number of international issues (such as US involvement in Vietnam). To achieve these aims, the Davignon Report recommended that an intergovernmental system of European Political Cooperation (EPC) be established to facilitate foreign policy harmonisation and coordination among member states. An emphasis on intergovernmental methods of operation ensured that the EPC sat outside the Community and was devoid of any supranational input (the Davignon Report deliberately avoided the establishment of a Secretariat that would manage foreign policy coordination). Coordination would be achieved principally through six-monthly meetings of foreign ministers (to be chaired by the Council Presidency), the establishment of a Political Committee (comprising the political directors of the national foreign ministries) and the linking of foreign ministries through a direct telex network.

Reaction to both reports was mixed among the Six. For France, EPC provided an important means of positioning Germany's increasingly active policy of *Ostpolitik* – which sought to establish relations with Eastern Europe – within the framework of the Community. And as the EPC (which was established in 1970) had an intergovernmental basis it did not threaten French national interests. The same could not be said for the Werner Report, which called for the creation of a monetary union over a ten-year period [*Doc.23*]. Such a process would not just involve the strengthening of economic policy cooperation among the member states. Decisions on interest rates, exchange rates and the management of reserves would be taken at the Community level. Fiscal harmonisation and cooperation on structural and regional policies would also have to take place, while various institutions would have to be created. Most obviously, this would include institutions to take decisions on economic policy and to coordinate the work of the central banks of the member states, while a direct implication of this was to further advance the cause of supranationalism.

Not all member states were willing to accept the further European integration that the proposal entailed. Whereas the German Chancellor, Willy Brandt, was supportive of the proposal, the French President, Georges Pompidou, showed no willingness to lend his support because of its supranational nature. In taking this decision, Pompidou was greatly influenced by the presence of continuing divisions between his government and the Gaullist Party on the key issue of supranationalism.

THE ENLARGED COMMUNITY

The consensus reached at the Hague summit on the principle of enlargement was followed by the start of substantive discussions in June 1970 with the four applicant states of Britain, Denmark, Ireland and Norway. By that stage the progress of the Community had been substantial: 1968 marked the completion of the customs union and a fully functioning agricultural policy. And although the integrative process suffered a setback with the 1966 Luxembourg Compromise, the Community's overall economic and political progress was a considerable draw for applicant states. This was particularly true for members of the European Free Trade Association, which was unable to offer an alternative to the economic and political strength of the Community.

Britain, which was now led by the Europhile Conservative Prime Minister Edward Heath, had come to the conclusion that neither the Commonwealth nor EFTA offered the advantages of market access and increased status that the Community did. The Heath government had been greatly influenced by the views of the business and banking community that membership was essential to revitalise Britain's economy. There had in effect occurred a waning of foreign policy options for Britain as the economic and political arguments for membership became impossible to ignore. 'Taking the years 1960–1970 as a whole, the GNP of "the Six" increased by an average of 4.2 per cent a year, compared with 2.3 per cent in Britain' (May, 1999: 41). Developments within the Community further improved the prospects for Britain joining. The Luxembourg Compromise's weakening of supranationalism [*Doc.20*] and the Yaoundé Convention's provision of guarantees to former colonies of the Six lessened Britain's concern about the adverse effect of the common external tariff on its preferential trading relations with the Commonwealth. Over and above these factors, it was Heath himself who greatly enhanced the prospects of Britain joining. He was deeply committed to the ideal of European unity and possessed none of the enthusiasm of his predecessors for the Commonwealth and the special relationship with the US. In practical terms, Heath's election as Prime Minister emphasised the refocusing of Britain's strategic priorities towards Europe. Yet it was a view that was not fully supported by the opposition Labour Party and as such Heath's act of faith in joining the Community did not mean that Britain's long-term commitment to the Community would be particularly straightforward.

Each of the applicants brought specific concerns to the membership negotiations, which in the case of Britain primarily related to Commonwealth trade, the cost of the CAP and the position of sterling. The overriding importance of joining the Community meant that British demands were considerably more modest than they had been in the previous two applications [*Docs 16 and 21*]. Heath was therefore a realist who understood that Britain's failure to engage in the ECSC and Treaty of Rome meant that there was a price to be paid for Community membership. For Britain, this 'price' would take the form of having to make significant contributions to the Community's budget, and the reality of this state of affairs was highlighted in the government White Papers of 1970 and 1971. Nonetheless, the common view among British negotiators at the time was that the impetus provided to the British economy through entry to the Community would in part offset this price.

Britain's application for Community membership was the determining factor that influenced the decision of the other applicants to follow its lead. As Ireland's economy was intrinsically linked to Britain's (approximately 70 per cent of Ireland's imports came from Britain and in excess of half of its exports went to Britain), it had little choice but to follow the British position. Nevertheless, policy-makers in Dublin hoped that Community membership would in the longer term help Ireland to become less dependent on Britain by developing economic and political links with a wider group of countries. Just as the economic and political benefits of membership were clear for Britain and Ireland, this was also true for Denmark and Norway and their strong economic links with Britain suggested that they should follow Britain's path. A key benefit of membership for Denmark was that it provided an increased market for its highly efficient agricultural sector. But despite the potential benefits of membership, both Denmark and Norway were suspicious of European involvement, having advocated the concept of Nordic unity since the end of the Second World War.

All in all, the major issues regarding membership for all four applicant nations were settled within a year, with discussions in the latter half of 1971 focusing on relatively minor issues. Of the four applicants, Britain was the only country not to hold a referendum on joining the Community: the decision to join was instead taken by Parliamentary vote. A referendum in Ireland produced an overwhelming majority of 83 per cent to 17 per cent in favour of membership, while in Denmark the vote was 63.3 per cent to 36.7 per cent in favour. This pattern would not be repeated in Norway, as its terms of membership were rejected in a popular referendum in September 1972 by 54.5 per cent to 45.5 per cent. Concerns over the necessity of international cooperation and the impact of Community membership on the agricultural industry had been paramount behind the Norwegian 'no' vote.

Although Norway's rejection of membership was a shock to the Community – it was the first time a state had rejected Community membership – it neither impeded the access of the other states nor adversely affected the EC's future. As a consequence, the Community grew to nine (and not ten) when Britain, Denmark and Ireland joined on 1 January 1973. The three new member states would add 60 million people to the EC, which in 1973 had a combined population of 250 million – a number broadly equivalent to the populations of the US and Soviet Union at that time. Just as the population of the Community was to increase, so too was its economic influence. The new member states would add to the EC's commercial standing (being broadly equivalent to the US and Japan) and would result in it accounting for one-fifth of world trade. Enlargement did, of course, reduce the membership and importance of EFTA, and with this in mind the applicant nations had emphasised the importance of establishing some form of special trading agreement between the EC and EFTA. The end product of these negotiations was a July 1972 agreement on a free trade area that would permit free trade among the nine EC countries and seven EFTA nations.

Even though it was clear that enlargement would enhance the EC's influence on world affairs, the future direction of an enlarged Community was less clear. The response to this question was once again to come from the French President, Georges Pompidou. He decided to convene a summit meeting of heads of state and government in October 1972 in Paris to examine how best to optimise the benefits of enlargement. As with the December 1969 Hague summit, Pompidou looked to the national leaders to map out the future path of European integration and in so doing provided additional evidence that the institutional pendulum had swung from the Commission towards the member states. It moreover confirmed the extent to which the Community had moved from the vision set out by the likes of Monnet.

Although they were technically not yet members of the Community, the applicant states took part in the summit meeting, which produced a number of agreements. This included a commitment to achieve the goal of Economic and Monetary Union (EMU) by 1980 (as had been set out in the Werner Report), the need to establish a common external trade policy towards the Soviet Union and Eastern Europe, and the need to make progress on a number of environmental, social and scientific matters. One of the most significant points to come from the meeting was agreement to develop a European Regional and Development Fund (ERDF) to promote economic and social cohesion. The ERDF – a proposal from Pompidou – was designed to provide the British Prime Minister, Edward Heath, with a positive European policy with which he could assuage domestic political criticism of Britain's entry to the Community to offset its minimal payments from the common agricultural policy. Thus, for some member states the ERDF helped to balance out the costs of EC membership. When working, the ERDF would provide financial aid for depressed industrial regions and Heath obviously hoped that such aid would lessen the cost – and reduce the criticism – of Britain's membership of the Community. In short, the Paris summit attempted to resolve potential problems and chart the future progress of the Community, as emphasised in the summit communiqué: 'The member states of the Community, the driving force of European construction, affirm their intention before the end of the present decade to transform the whole complex of their relations into a European Union.'

As the Community approached 1973, its future appeared bright. 'Three years after the Hague summit,' John Young has written, 'the Community seemed on the brink, not merely of a major enlargement but of a leap towards full economic union' (Young, 1991: 46). This was not to happen. The Werner Report's goal of establishing economic and monetary union by 1980 was undermined by instability in the international economy. One reason for this volatility was the US decision to cut interest rates in May 1971 and the decision a few months later on 15 August 1971 to suspend the dollar convertibility. In response to the increasingly precarious international financial system, Community member states attempted to inject a degree of stability into European economies in April 1972 by agreeing to restrict currency fluctuations. It would be achieved by a system of currency cooperation – the Snake – that would restrict the fluctuations of EC currencies within a 2.5 per cent boundary inside a 'tunnel' [*Doc.25*]. But while the six EC members of the Snake were joined in May 1972 by Britain and Denmark, the new participants' involvement was only temporary: both withdrew one month later, while Italy's membership was terminated in February 1973.

The inability of participants to stay within the Snake was the product of a difficult international economic situation that spawned rising unemployment and high levels of inflation. Economic conditions were made worse by the

October 1973 Arab–Israeli War that was immediately followed by soaring oil prices. In an effort to grapple with these developments, a European Monetary Cooperation Fund was set up in 1973 to provide additional support to weak currencies, although it was of limited worth. Concerned about the ongoing economic difficulties, Pompidou yet again called for a meeting of heads of government, to be held this time in Copenhagen in December 1973. Faced with a chronic international economic climate, the leaders of the (now) nine member states failed to reach agreement on how best to respond. The meeting proved worthless, producing no initiatives to assist EC economies, and was immediately followed by the French withdrawal from the Snake on 19 January 1974. And although France rejoined the Snake in July 1975, it was forced to withdraw for a second time in March 1976 and by then the very existence of the Snake looked increasingly precarious. The economic conditions that undermined the Snake also damaged the potential of achieving monetary union. Indeed, as early as 1975 a European Commission report would emphasise that 'Europe is no nearer to EMU than in 1969. In fact, if there has been any movement, it has been backward' (Marjolin *et al.*, 1975: 1). As a consequence, interest in the Snake lessened and member states buried any hopes of achieving monetary union by 1980.

BRITAIN'S INDECISION

International economic difficulties were one of two main problems that impacted on Community progress in the 1970s. The other concerned Britain. In the British general election of February 1974, Harold Wilson's Labour Party defeated the Conservative government and as a result Wilson once again occupied the position of Prime Minister. Labour's victory was achieved partly on the back of a campaign that sought to renegotiate the terms of entry to the Community that Heath had obtained. In truth, however, the commitment to renegotiate was as much influenced by the need to pacify the deep divisions within the Labour Party on European issues as it was by the need to appease the electorate. Scepticism within the Labour Party on European matters had increased in the wake of Wilson's failed application for membership in November 1967. Concerns over threats to sovereignty, the impact on the Commonwealth and fears over higher prices all helped to fuel Labour Party scepticism on European matters. Along with his foreign secretary, James Callaghan, Wilson set about the process of renegotiating the terms of entry. As with many other issues, Wilson was pragmatic on the question of Europe and possessed none of the pro-European credentials of Heath. Callaghan, by contrast, was rather more sceptical and was publicly willing to question the value of Britain's membership of the Community. In making the case for renegotiation, Wilson was aware that his leadership of a minority government could come unstuck over Europe. And although there were notable supporters of European integration within the Labour Party (such as Roy Jenkins and David Owen), a significant proportion of the rank and file of the party were sceptical and the renegotiation was thus aimed at reconciling divisions between those who were against membership and those who wanted Britain to remain in the Community. The process of renegotiation was thus part of Wilson's strategy to maintain unity within the Labour Party and was regarded by many to be a 'superficial exercise'. The former British Ambassador to Germany, Nicholas Henderson, has written that Wilson '. . . did not seem to see himself in any creative political role. He was quite frank . . . about his main objective, which was to keep all the clashing balls of the Labour Party in the air at the same time' (Henderson, 1994: 72).

Having been entrusted with the responsibility of dealing with the renegotiations, Callaghan managed at his first Council meeting in April 1974 to irritate his fellow foreign ministers by informing them of Britain's demands. Even though the government stressed that the renegotiations hinged on seven points, many were of little relevance. 'Labour's manifesto had promised to retain a zero VAT rate on basic items, but EC rules *did* not obstruct this; neither did the EC prevent Britain from protecting its balance of payments by limiting capital movements with Europe; and the Labour party's criticism of EMU was pointless because EMU was no longer in the realm of practical politics' (Young: 2000: 113). This meant that the renegotiations were dominated by four key issues: extending the Yaoundé Convention to assist Commonwealth and other third world exporters; reforming the CAP to lower food prices and help third world producers; ensuring that the Commission would not interfere with Britain's industrial and regional policies; and readjusting Britain's budgetary contributions. Some of the issues were more difficult than others.

Britain's desire to assist Commonwealth and other third world countries chimed with a general viewpoint that the Community should do more to improve its relations with the third world. It would lead in a matter of months to the February 1975 Lomé Convention which helped to protect the exports of developing countries by exempting them from tariffs and providing them with various guaranteed quotas. Other issues proved more difficult to resolve. Britain's desire to reform the CAP made little headway as the new French President, Valery Giscard d'Estaing (who succeeded Pompidou after his death in May 1974), was unwilling to adjust a policy that favoured French farmers. Discussions over the Community budget were the most difficult and for Britain were not helped by a May 1974 Treasury report which forecasted that by 1980 it would be responsible for 24 per cent of the EC budget despite accounting for only 14 per cent of the Community's gross national product.

In the end it would take two summit meetings before agreement could be reached on the terms of Britain's renegotiations at Dublin in March 1975. Prior to that meeting, the Paris summit of December 1974 produced agreement on the exact size of the ERDF: Britain would receive 28 per cent of all funding, while France, Ireland and Italy would also obtain significant support. The ERDF – which Heath had argued for in the accession negotiations – provided Wilson with an opportunity to demonstrate to his critics that Britain was 'getting something back'. The Paris summit was significant for producing agreement on a 'corrective mechanism' which would ensure that Britain, or for that matter any member state, would not pay too much into the EC budget. The summit also took the opportunity to resolve a number of issues that were unrelated to the renegotiations. These included the principle of direct elections to the European Parliament (the first of which took place in 1979) and the taking of a decision to commission the Belgian Prime Minister, Leo Tindemans, to provide a report on European union. When published in December 1975, the Tindemans Report contained little to satisfy those who hoped it would lead to a federal Europe. It focused instead on institutional reform and the further widening of the Community's activities (as in the field of foreign and security policy) and outlined a proposal for the creation of a two-speed Europe in which the degree of integration would depend on the willingness and ability of member states to cooperate. Not surprisingly, this was unacceptable to many of the smaller member states and, combined with other concerns over the erosion of sovereignty, led to the Tindemans Report being silenced [*Doc.27*].

By far the most significant development at Paris was the recognition of the important role that summits had come to play in the Community's progress. Member states thus reached agreement that such summits would in future take the form of a European Council, whose first meeting would take place in Dublin in March 1975. It would comprise heads of government, with the President of the Commission being given the right to attend. In terms of operation, it would meet three times a year (changed to twice a year in 1985) and be led by a member state that would assume the role of the 'Presidency of the European Council', which would rotate among the member states on a six-monthly basis [*Doc.26*]. The future of European integration would therefore greatly depend on the decisions taken by heads of government at European Council 'summits' and the nature of relationships among the member states. This particularly applied to the Franco–German axis. After the difficulties of the early 1970s, a particularly close relationship was formed between French President Giscard d'Estaing and the German Chancellor Helmut Schmidt (both of whom came to office in 1974), which lasted for the rest of the decade.

Apart from the symbolic nature of the March 1975 Dublin European Council, it was noteworthy for finally producing agreement on the outstanding issues of Britain's renegotiations. This included the nature of the 'corrective mechanism' whereby a rebate would be given to any net contributor state that met a rather complex Commission formula. For this to happen a member state would have to meet certain criteria that related to its balance of payments, growth rate and share of gross national product (GNP). The exact nature of the rebate would be two-thirds of the difference between its share of GNP and its budget contributions, although not more than its total VAT contributions. In the end, however, the renegotiations did little to assist Britain in building a fruitful relationship with other member states, who regarded it as an 'unreliable partner in Europe' (Henderson, 1994: 66). According to Roy Jenkins, President of the European Commission at the time, the whole process 'produced the minimum results with the maximum ill-will' (Jenkins, 1991: 375). It is a point echoed by Roy Denman, who considered that it produced 'the minimum of gain for the maximum of irritation' (Denman, 1996: 250). Having been a member of the Community for just over a year, the process of renegotiation severely impacted on Britain's status in the Community and raised suspicions within the Community about British membership.

Domestically, the renegotiated terms did little to ease the divisions within the Labour Party. This was despite the fact that the terms received majority support from the Cabinet, which voted 16 to 7 in their favour on 17 March 1975. The House of Commons too offered its support on 9 April by 398 votes to 172 in favour. Thus, having received this endorsement, Wilson started the process of holding a referendum on the renegotiated terms. Yet because the Labour Party – and moreover the Cabinet – was far from united on the question of Europe, Wilson dropped the established practice of collective responsibility and permitted government ministers to exercise their own decision. When the membership referendum eventually took place in June 1975, the terms were supported by approximately 2 to 1 of the voters: 17.3 million people voted in favour and 8.4 million against. Many would be forgiven for thinking that the outcome of the renegotiation and referendum would be to settle once and for all the question of British membership. This was not to happen. Many individuals within the Labour Party continued to argue against EC membership, including withdrawal from the Community (a policy that the party committed itself to in the 1983 general election). At a broader level, the renegotiated terms had failed to rectify fully the level of Britain's budget contributions. This was starkly emphasised by a government calculation that Britain would be the largest net contributor to the Community budget by 1978, despite being ranked fifth in terms of its share of the Community's gross domestic product.

EUROSCLEROSIS

The history of renegotiation, referendum and budgetary dispute did little to enhance Britain's status within the Community. If anything it confirmed its status as 'an awkward partner'. British indecision was, however, not the primary reason for the difficulties that beset the Community in the 1970s. The progress anticipated at the 1969 Hague summit had been hampered by the unwillingness of member states to support new initiatives at a time of international economic instability. At the same time, the supranational institutions of the Community, particularly the European Commission, had appeared to be unable to deal with the challenges that the Community faced. And although the appointment of Roy Jenkins as President of the European Commission in 1977 – after François Ortoli's lacklustre presidency – appeared to signal a renewed sense of purpose and dynamism in the Community's activities, for all intents and purposes the Community's fortunes had not been substantially revived by the early 1980s. In part, the Commission's lack of purpose was influenced by the legacy of de Gaulle and his efforts to reduce the influence of the supranational institutions.

Despite the general malaise that dominated the decade, there were some notable developments. These included the decision of the Paris summit of 1974 to establish the European Council and confirm the principle of direct elections to the European Parliament [*Doc.26*]. Both decisions had a lasting impact on the future progress of the Community. The creation of the European Council, which comprised the heads of state and government of the member states and which was led by a presidency that rotated among the national governments on a six-monthly basis, institutionalised the practice of summitry [*Doc.26*]. As such, it also emphasised a decline in the importance of the supranational influence of the Commission and an increase in the importance of intergovernmental relations. But while this state of affairs pleased the member states, it also raised the question as to how the Community would be able to deal adequately with future challenges in the absence of strong leadership. This included the prospect of enlargement; applications were received from Greece in 1975 and Portugal and Spain in 1979.

In contrast to the immediate impact that the European Council had on European integration, the European Parliament's influence was not substantially altered in the immediate term by the decision to elect its membership in future by direct election. The European Parliament continued to remain a relatively weak institution, in the eyes of both the electorate and the member state governments. This was not least influenced by the general lack of support for the elections – Britain had the noteworthy status of having had fewer people vote as a percentage of the population than elsewhere in the EC [*Doc.40*]. The first direct elections to the European Parliament of 1979 were therefore not part of a wider process of reform and its influence on the decision-making process changed only when the Single European Act and subsequent Treaty on European Union revised the decision-making procedures that had initially been established in the Treaty of Rome.

Just as the holding of direct elections did not immediately transform the Community's fortunes, the same could be said for the decision to establish the European Monetary System (EMS) in March 1979 [*Doc.28*]. On his appointment as President of the European Commission in 1977, Jenkins' desire to inject a fresh sense of purpose in the Community had been emphasised by his wish to reproclaim 'the goal of monetary union' that had been outlined initially in the October 1970 Werner Report [*Doc.23*]. Under the leadership of Giscard and Schmidt, France and Germany were once again supportive of this goal: they argued in favour of creating a fixed exchange rate that linked European currencies as a means of overcoming the economic difficulties of the 1970s and in particular the instability created by the US devaluation of the dollar. Support for the EMS was to be found among other member states and as such demonstrated a change in the underlying political climate that once again emphasised further integration in this area of policy-making. The EMS, which was made up of a European currency unit (ECU) and an Exchange Rate Mechanism (ERM), was regarded as a way of reducing exchange rate instability and as a means of combating the divergent inflation rates that were prevalent in European economies in the late 1970s. Yet while it managed to provide stability by the mid-1980s, its early years of operation were subject to significant instability, with not all member states willing to participate (including Britain).

In all, the combined difficulties that the EC encountered during the 1970s have led to the decade being categorised as a 'dark age' of European integration. Just as internal factors – such as the leadership qualities of the European Commission – and external developments – such as the oil crisis – lay at the root of the difficulties of the 1970s, the ability of the Community to progress beyond this stagnation in European integration would be determined by internal and external circumstances. Yet, for all intents and purposes, the initial years of the 1980s did not signal a dramatic change in the Community's fortunes, thereby leading some commentators to conclude that the limit of European integration had been reached.

CHAPTER FIVE

RENEWED PROGRESS: 1980–89

For much of the 1970s a range of factors hampered the European Community's progress. This included a downturn in the international economy that was exacerbated by the 1973–74 and 1979–80 oil crises and the difficulty of integrating new members (particularly Britain). At the same time, the Community's institutions appeared to be too weak to deal with these challenges. It was therefore hoped that the 1980s would result in a revival of the EC's fortunes by marking an end to the period of Eurosclerosis that had dominated the 1970s.

At first sight, the prospects for renewed progress appeared promising. 1979 was witness to the first direct elections to the European Parliament and the creation of the European Monetary System [*Doc.28*]. Two years later the Community's membership expanded to ten with the accession of Greece which, along with Portugal and Spain (who joined in 1986), would form what would be regarded as the Mediterranean enlargement. But far from overturning the fortunes of the Community, little progress took place during the first four years of the decade. For the most part, the Community continued to rest in the doldrums. One of the factors that limited the Community's ability to move beyond this sluggish progress was the lack of leadership provided by the Commission. And although the Commission's fortunes had improved under Roy Jenkins's presidency (1977–81), his successor, Gaston Thorn (1981–84), proved to be a largely ineffectual leader. The protracted struggle over the level of Britain's contributions to the Community budget proved to be the other significant factor in limiting the Community's progress [*Doc.30*]. As a consequence, the combination of the resolution of the budget dispute at the June 1984 Fontainebleau European Council and the appointment of the more dynamic Jacques Delors as President of the European Commission in 1985 would assist the Community in moving forward on a path of renewed integration. At the same time the combined desire of the Commission and some member states to establish stronger EC policies helped to create a climate that was increasingly favourable to institutional and policy change. All in all, this led directly to the creation of a single European market that in turn prompted closer cooperation in a number of other areas, such as social policy, and which would in time lead to the design and establishment of a single European currency.

TRANSATLANTIC DIFFICULTIES

'The EC's external relations', Desmond Dinan has written, 'were every bit as problematical as its internal development in the early 1980s' (Dinan, 1999: 96). This was the result of two linked but distinct factors. First, in the wake of the period of détente that had dominated the 1970s, the emergence of a second cold war in the early 1980s raised serious questions about the ability of the Community to react to the changed international environment through the intergovernmental European Political Cooperation framework that had been established in 1970 [*Doc.24*]. This was because, despite the fact that the intergovernmental nature of EPC reflected the determination of member states to maintain national control over foreign policy, the absence of provision for majority voting and the lack of a permanent secretariat at times led to difficulties in establishing a united policy. Second, Ronald Reagan took office as President of the United States in 1981 with the aim of restoring US military and political strength, particularly vis-à-vis the Soviet Union. But EC member states for the most part did not share this view as they were attempting to create a working relationship between themselves and the Soviets.

Nowhere was this change in US policy more apparent than in the area of nuclear weapons. The Reagan administration launched the Strategic Defence Initiative (SDI) in 1983 to protect America from Soviet attack. The implication of such a policy was perfectly clear: the principle of equal security (and equal vulnerability) which had formed the bed-rock of NATO would have been reduced as the US obtained greater protection than its allies. Europeans responded angrily: as they saw it, the US was abandoning them and protecting its own interests. Helmut Schmidt noted this view when he said that 'today there is a growing tendency in the United States to focus on its own national interests as it perceives them; at present there prevails almost a kind of euphoria about American vigour and strength, which is reflected in current American arms and military policy. And, frankly, these attitudes are disturbing to Europeans' (Schmidt, 1985: 59). As evidence of this divergence of views, in 1982 the United States imposed sanctions on US companies and licence holders involved in the construction of a 3,600-mile Soviet gas pipeline which was designed to export Soviet gas from the Western Siberian Urengoy gas field to Western Europe. Concerned about the possibility of job losses through a loss of contracts, European governments were angered by the hypocrisy of the Reagan administration which continued to sell grain to the Soviet Union while seeking to block the pipeline.

A combination of the intergovernmental nature of EPC and a divergence of views with the United States resulted in a renewed effort among Community member states to develop stronger forms of foreign policy cooperation. This included the October 1981 London Report, the 1981 Genscher-Colombo Plan, the 1983 Stuttgart Solemn Declaration and the 1984 European Parliament's Draft Treaty establishing the European Union (the Spinnelli Plan). At the same time that EC member states wanted to improve the effectiveness of their foreign policy cooperation by further developing EPC, they sought to 'reactivate' the Western European Union as a way of countering the dominance that the US exercised in foreign and security policy and in East–West relations. Thus, as the United States was the dominant force in NATO, EC member states viewed the WEU as an organisation in which they could discuss their differing views from the United States. All in all, these developments demonstrated that there was considerable support among member states to make changes to the institutional design of the Community, not least in the area of foreign policy because of the changed geopolitical environment. But before such changes could take place, the Community would have to resolve the outstanding question of Britain's budget contributions.

BRITAIN'S BUDGETARY QUESTION

After the difficulties that had engulfed Britain's membership of the European Community under the Labour governments of the late 1970s, there was a genuine hope within Britain that the election of a Conservative government led by Margaret Thatcher in May 1979 would produce a more positive British attitude towards European integration. Such an outlook was influenced by the fact that the Conservatives had consistently been the 'Party of Europe' and that Thatcher had herself supported a continuance of Britain's membership of the Community at the time of the 1975 referendum. It was a false hope. In government Thatcher failed to establish the positive policy that had been expected and instead deployed a combative style of leadership on European issues.

Thatcher's support for Europe was based on practical grounds rather than as a result of some form of deep-seated bond. She followed the path taken by the majority of Britain's post-war prime ministers who (apart from Edward Heath) viewed European matters as part of a cost–benefit analysis. She realised the importance that EC membership meant for the British economy in terms of market access and as a means of creating and sustaining employment opportunities through inward investment. The Community's position as the world's largest trading bloc enhanced Britain's international role. At a time of renewed cold war tension she understood the political role that the Community played in uniting a large number of European countries against the Soviet Union. But despite the evident benefits of membership, she believed that there should be clear limits to the Community's influence and that key decisions should continue to rest with the member states. It was a viewpoint that would in a short period of time create a significant division between Britain and her European partners.

Without doubt the key issue that dominated the early years of the Thatcher government was the British budget question [*Doc.30*]. Commonly referred to as the 'Bloody British Question' in Brussels, it was an issue that Harold Wilson had been unable to resolve satisfactorily at the time of the 1974 renegotiation of Britain's membership. The 1975 rebate mechanism that derived from the renegotiations failed to overturn Britain's status as one of the main net contributors to the Community budget (the other being Germany) and when combined with the escalating costs of the common agricultural policy ensured that the question of Britain's budget contributions remained a key issue for British negotiators. Britain received little funding from the CAP because British farmers tended to be more efficient than continental farmers, as well as concentrating in such areas as sheep farming that were not as generously subsidised. By the end of the transitional period of adjustment in January 1978, the British Treasury predicted that Britain would be the largest net contributor to the budget, with a projected deficit of £1 billion for 1979–80, despite Britain's income being less than the EC average. In short, Britain was paying too much into the Community budget and receiving too little out.

Thatcher lost no time in attempting to address the budget imbalance in a number of informal meetings with the French President, German Chancellor and Italian Prime Minister. For the most part, the discussions resulted in little concrete progress and although the German Chancellor, Helmut Schmidt, was broadly sympathetic to Britain's plight given that Germany was the other net contributor, its economic strength nevertheless ensured that the budget contributions did not overly worry Germany. Having not got very far in these informal meetings, Thatcher managed to put the budget question 'squarely on the [EC] agenda' when, according to her, she 'spelt out the facts' at the June 1979 Strasbourg European Council (Thatcher, 1993: 64). But while Thatcher thought that she 'had made an impression as someone who meant business', the then President of the European Commission, Roy Jenkins, reflected that she 'performed the considerable feat of unnecessarily irritating two big countries, three small ones and the Commission with her opening performance at a European Council' (Thatcher, 1993: 64; Jenkins, 1991: 495). A few months later, in October 1979, Thatcher stressed that Britain could not accept the existing situation on the Community budget because it was 'demonstrably unjust' and it signified a tougher negotiating position on her part. Although Britain's partners were by that stage more willing to acknowledge the presence of a serious problem, they were unwilling to accept the argument that Britain's payments to the budget should be approximately equivalent to what it received from the Community. But instead of producing a diplomatic breakthrough, Thatcher's style of diplomacy served only to cement the position of the other member states which were unwilling to accept the British demands.

Faced with this criticism Thatcher stood steadfast in campaigning for a budget rebate; in her eyes 'Britain was asking no more than its due' (Thatcher, 1993: 81). As part of an effort to deflate the argument, the Commission proposed at the Dublin meeting that Britain receive a rebate of £350 million along with the promise that Britain would in future obtain more direct Community funding. But for Thatcher it was an unacceptable offer and the failure to provide the full rebate of £1 billion ensured that the Council meeting broke up without agreement [*Doc.30*]. This strategy of holding firm ensured that the budget question dominated the Community agenda for some time to come, despite the presence of many other vital issues to which the member states needed to respond. This included domestic economic recession, unemployment and an unstable international environment that was marked by the renewed cold war conflict and the 1979 Soviet invasion of Afghanistan.

Britain's insistence that it would block any issues until the budget question was resolved antagonised the other member states which contemplated excluding Britain from new EC initiatives as a means of moving beyond the deadlock. But Thatcher was also just as tired with the budgetary battle and had come to the conclusion that the time was drawing near to settle the debate, with a solution finally being reached at the June 1984 Fontainebleau European Council. The agreement provided Britain with an immediate lump-sum payment of 1000 million ECU for 1984, while in subsequent years it would receive a rebate amounting to two-thirds of the difference between what it contributed in VAT and what it received from the Community budget. The settlement also led to Britain agreeing to a general increase in EC revenue from 1 per cent to 1.4 per cent of national VAT receipts in order to remedy a general deficit in budgetary resources. But at what price had Prime Minister Thatcher secured a budget rebate? Even though the financial sums involved were sizeable, they were not considerably more than what had been available in previous months and when put into a national context were even smaller: the entire EC budget was equivalent at that time to the expenditure of a large British department of state and in total accounted for approximately 1 per cent of the national income of member states. Moreover, the Fontainebleau deal did not settle Britain's concerns over the EC budget once and for all: the agreement could be subject to a future review and it did not prevent the possibility of further increases in the budget. More importantly, while Thatcher presented the budget dispute as a means of defending Britain's national sovereignty, by 1984 Britain was far more closely integrated with the Community than it had been when she was elected Prime Minister in 1979.

CREATING THE SINGLE MARKET

In the early 1980s there was a growing consensus among member states and the EU institutions about the need to foster renewed European integration. A

'Declaration on European Union' was presented at the June 1983 Stuttgart European Council and while it proved to be of little value, it was demonstrative of a climate of change. At the same time, the Community was faced with a decline in its economic competitiveness, which by 1982 had fallen dramatically behind that of Japan and the United States. American and Japanese companies had established a dominant position in the new technologies of semiconductors and consumer electronics. This state of affairs prompted the European Commission, member states and business interest groups jointly to advocate the implementation of initiatives that would improve the economic competitiveness of the Community. This particularly applied to the creation of a single market.

The objective of a single market could be traced back to the Treaty of Rome: Article 2 stipulated that 'The Community shall have as its aim, by establishing a common market and progressively approximating the economic policies of member states, to promote throughout the Community a harmonious development of economic activities, a continuous and balanced expansion, an increase in stability, an accelerated raising of the standard of living and closer relations between its member states' [*Doc.15*]. But despite the initial progress that the Community had made in the 1960s, the objective of creating a 'common market' had become bogged down from the late 1960s until the early 1980s. For the majority of that period, member states had faced economic difficulties that led national governments to adopt inward-looking policies that were prompted by a desire to protect domestic jobs from foreign competition.

In practical terms this meant that, although the process of European integration had brought the member states together by, among other factors, increasing the number of cross-border tourist flows within Europe, which increased from 40 million cross-frontier arrivals in 1960 to over 160 million in 1980, there nevertheless remained significant barriers which hindered the Community's competitiveness. In this sense, the concept of a single market based on the free movement of workers, goods and the mutual recognition of products did not exist. It was a point that had in fact been most notably highlighted in the European Court of Justice's (ECJ) 1979 *Cassis de Dijon* ruling which tackled a German ban on the importation of alcoholic beverages from other member states that did not meet minimum German alcohol contents [*Doc.29*]. In responding to this situation, the Court ruled that 'There is therefore no valid reason why, provided that they have been lawfully produced and marketed in one of the Member States, alcoholic beverages should not be introduced into any other Member State; the sale of such products may not be subject to a legal prohibition on the marketing of beverages with an alcohol content lower than the limit set by the national rules' [*Doc.29*]. While the Court's decision noted the principle of mutual recognition, the ruling did not result in the imposition of a policy that advocated the mutual recognition of product standards. The ECJ's ability to tackle questions that related to market access was moreover wholly dependent on cases that were lodged and the Court therefore could not be relied upon to make whole-scale change. As a consequence, individual member states continued to exercise their ability to ban the importation of certain goods. France ignored the Court's decision by banning lamb imports in 1980, while ecological concerns prompted Denmark to prohibit the sale of beer and soft drinks unless they were sold in recyclable containers.

Such examples were symptomatic of a broader trend that developed in the 1970s for member states to protect their domestic markets at a time of economic downturn. In a climate of high inflation and soaring unemployment, Community law prohibited member states from protecting their industrial sectors from the competition of other member states through the use of quotas and tariff barriers. Faced with this situation, national governments utilised a plethora of non-tariff barriers to trade to protect their domestic markets. This included the use of regulations and the granting of subsidies. Yet the use of non-tariff barriers by member states to protect domestic employment levels had a direct impact on the competitiveness of the EC as a whole because the use of subsidies helped to sustain high-cost production as companies were sheltered from wider market competition. Such a course of action arguably represented a retreat from, rather than an advance towards, a common market; there continued to exist a number of barriers that hindered the concept of the free movement of goods, peoples or services among the member states. This state of affairs was moreover reflected in a slowdown in the growth of intra-European trade.

The advances that had been made by many of the Community's main trading partners compounded the lack of improvements in the economic competitiveness of EC member states. The Community was faced with increasing levels of imports from the United States and Japan and a number of newly industrialising countries that included Hong Kong and Taiwan. And as the poor competitiveness of the EC limited its number of exports, the Community as a whole experienced large trade deficits. This situation was made worse by evidence that the Community's ability to attract and sustain inward investment, particularly from the United States, was declining. Business groups, which were increasingly organised on a European-wide basis, were particularly concerned about the Community's lack of competitiveness that they rightly perceived to be strongly influenced by the presence of non-tariff barriers to trade. National governments too were worried about levels of competitiveness, a situation that was strongly influenced by the election of a number of right-of-centre governments in Belgium, Denmark, Italy, the Netherlands and Britain. West Germany's coalition of Free Democrats and Christian Democrats was also supportive of market reform. There was consequently a convergence of national interests, with many Community member states sharing similar goals of free competition. National governments – particularly Britain, Germany and the Netherlands – and business lobby groups were united in their desire to develop a single market as a means of improving the economic performance of the Community and narrowing the technological gap with the United States and Japan.

In the early 1980s these concerns were reflected in a number of developments, including the communiqués of the European Council and in the work of the European Round Table of Industrialists, which lobbied for the completion of the single market. The European Round Table, which comprised a mixture of public and private representatives, including the then European Commissioner for Industry, Etienne Davignon, was influential in the establishment in 1982 of the ESPRIT programme for cross-border European co-operation in information technology. However, it was not until the June 1984 Fontainebleau European Council that significant progress was made towards the creation of a single market. Having resolved the problem of Britain's budget contributions, the Fontainebleau meeting moved on to the question of institutional reform and the development of the single market. The first question of institutional reform had been influenced by the European Parliament's approval in February 1984 of the Draft Treaty on European Union which, under the leadership of the Italian Euro-federalist Altiero Spinelli, had called for the negotiation of a new treaty to replace the existing treaties. The second question of the single market received significant endorsement from the member states, illustrated when the British government tabled a proposal at the Fontainebleau European Council for the creation of a genuine 'common market' in goods and services which signalled a more positive British approach to the EC.

To take some of these matters forward, the Fontainebleau meeting established two ad-hoc committees to examine the future of European integration. One committee was to be chaired by Jim Dooge (an Irish senator), with the remit of focusing on institutional matters, while the other, chaired by Pietro Adonnino (an Italian parliamentarian), would examine the possibility of creating a 'People's Europe'. Of these committees, the Adonnino committee presented a number of proposals for a Citizen's Europe that in the short term proved to have little impact on the Community. The same could not be said for the Dooge committee. Its conclusions, which were presented to the Brussels European Council of March 1985, recommended a strengthening of Community institutions (including a more effective role for the European Parliament), an end to the use of the national veto in EC decision-making and the creation of a single European market.

Parallel to these developments, a new Commission entered office at the start of 1985 under the presidency of Jacques Delors who set out a swift plan of action for reforming the Community with the goal of completing an internal market and therefore eliminating the Community's internal frontiers by the end of 1992. This desire for a grand policy was evocative of Jenkins' pursuance of the European Monetary System; Delors' appointment marked a sea change in the institutional make-up of the Community, with the Commission becoming a 'policy entrepreneur' whereby it acted as a key initiator of policy. Delors argued that if there were to be a genuine single market, there would have to be an increase in supranationalism so that national economic interests could not hamper the development of the Community. The Commission's influence in shaping the single market agenda mirrored neo-functional accounts and contrasted with intergovernmentalist arguments that the single market was the product of a convergence of member states' policy preferences. In reality, however, various factors interacted, including the Commission's policy leadership role and a convergence of national interests.

The combination of the convergence of member states' views, interest group pressure, Delors' vision and the Dooge committee's findings resulted in EC leaders asking the European Commission at the March 1985 Brussels European Council to establish a plan that would result in the creation of a genuine 'single market'. This task was given to the British Internal Market Commissioner, Lord Arthur Cockfield, and the ensuing White Paper, *Completing the Internal Market*, set out nearly 300 measures that would be necessary to achieve the removal of all internal barriers within the Community to enable the free movement of people, services, capital and goods by 1992 (Cockfield, 1994). But while such a proposal mirrored British interests, it was also true that for it to be effective the Commission would have to set in motion a process of harmonisation of national regulations. At the same time, the Commission would have to take on the responsibility for managing and 'policing' the single market. The underlying implication of Cockfield's proposals was perfectly clear: it would lead to a dramatic increase in the supranational power of the Commission and lessen the influence of the member states.

In advancing the case for the single market, the Commission argued that the progress of the Community was hindered by the presence of fiscal, physical and technical barriers. Fiscal barriers related to the different levels of value-added tax that existed among member states, which the Commission argued was a central factor in influencing the presence of frontier controls. This was because member states used frontier controls to stop the importation of goods – such as cigarettes and alcohol – from a state with a lower tax rate into a state with a higher rate. To remedy this situation, the Commission proposed that value-added tax rates should be harmonised into two rates of 14–20 per cent and 4–9 per cent. In contrast to fiscal barriers, physical barriers related to the custom and immigration controls; the Commission argued that their presence placed a heavy burden on business and therefore proposed that they should be abolished (a policy that was particularly attractive to many Europeans). The final category of technical barriers concerned the technical regulations and standards that differed in each of the member states and as such ensured that it was quite likely for a product that met the requirements of one country to be unacceptable to another. To remedy this state of affairs the Commission proposed a harmonisation of member states' regulations based on the principle of mutual recognition which had been initially highlighted in the 1979 *Cassis de Dijon* case and which would be confirmed in the Single European Act [*Doc.29*]. In all, the Commission's proposals for the creation of a single market were clearly of a substantial nature, but for them to be effective it would also be necessary to reform the process of decision-making within the Community.

THE SINGLE EUROPEAN ACT

At the Milan European Council of June 1985 the heads of government of the member states discussed the Commission's White Paper (for completion of the single market by 1992) and the Dooge Report's proposals for institutional reform, the latter of which advocated a reduction in the use of the national veto in Community decision-making. The gathering consensus behind the need for institutional reform was further shaped by the concerns of existing members about the impact of enlarging the EC. Greece had joined in January 1981 and the Community agreed in June 1984 that Portugal and Spain would join in January 1986. The imminent nature of the EC's enlargement raised questions about whether it would be possible to achieve agreement among the national governments in a Community of 12 member states. The prospect of prolonged discussions and unresolved questions thus prompted member states to consider the use of majority voting for the taking of decisions.

The combination of the single market programme, the Dooge Report on institutional reform and the enlargement of the Community led a number of member states to advocate that to tackle fully these issues a new treaty should be negotiated in an intergovernmental conference (IGC). But as some member states – particularly Britain – did not support the need for holding an IGC, the chairman of the Milan European Council, Italy's Bettino Craxi, took the extraordinary step of calling for a majority vote on the IGC. Of the ten member states, only Britain, Denmark and Greece voted against, having argued that there was no need for institutional reforms. It was, however, a view that was not shared by the majority of member states, which agreed to the holding of the IGC. Such an outcome further complicated the position of Britain, Denmark and Greece because their opposition had failed to stop the Community's development. Faced with this state of affairs, they could, of course, have boycotted the IGC. Yet it was an unrealistic objective because the combined significance of the talks and the importance of the Community to each of their economies meant that they had no option but to participate and be bound by the results. For Thatcher, the situation was all the more galling because the single market programme had been greatly influenced by her efforts. She later commented, 'I had witnessed a profound shift in how European policy was conducted – and therefore in the kind of Europe that was taking shape. A Franco–German bloc with its own agenda had re-emerged to set the direction of the Community' (Thatcher, 1993: 558–9). But despite this opposition, there was nonetheless a tacit acknowledgement within the British government that the continuing use of the national veto ensured that any member state would have the ability to slow down the single market programme.

The IGC negotiations commenced in September 1985 and culminated in agreement on a Single European Act (SEA) at the Luxembourg European Council of December 1985 [*Doc.31*]. The SEA was the first major revision of the Community since the 1957 Treaty of Rome and was concerned as much with implementing new policies and decision-making procedures as it was with formally recognising policies that had developed since 1957. The latter included the Regional Development Fund and European Political Cooperation. At the same time, the SEA extended the Community's competence into a number of new areas, including environmental, social and technological policies. These developments, such as the provision of a legal base for environmental policy in the SEA, demonstrated both a shift in the focus of the Community's attention to areas of policy that had traditionally rested with member states (with decisions, such as those on environment, to be taken by qualified majority voting) and a strengthening of the Commission's legislative and regulative role within the Community. This would in turn lead the Commission to play a stronger role in many international negotiations. Such activity pointed to the growing role that the Community played as a global actor, having an input on international policy ranging from economics and trade to environmental and development cooperation. The changing nature of the European policy process also meant that the Community became a far more attractive venue for interest groups to engage in lobbying activities that centred on the European Commission.

Apart from these developments, the SEA impacted on the role of the European Parliament which, despite its position as a democratically elected body (since 1979), had played a relatively minor role in the policy-making process. Set against this background, Germany and Italy were two of the most vociferous member states that argued that the European Parliament's powers needed to be strengthened so as to increase the democratic legitimacy of the Community. Britain opposed such a development because it represented a federalist view of European integration. France also opposed increasing the European Parliament's powers. Despite this opposition, an agreement was eventually reached at the December 1985 Luxembourg European Council on the SEA which included an augmentation in the European Parliament's influence. (The SEA only came into effect on 1 July 1987 because of the difficulty of getting it ratified in the member states.) As a result of this agreement, the European Parliament's powers were increased through the introduction of a new cooperation procedure which ensured that it would be fully involved in the legislative process, including the majority of the single market directives. In addition to these changes to the role of the European Commission and the European Parliament, the other major institutional reform introduced by the SEA concerned the introduction of qualified majority voting within the Council of Ministers. Despite concern among some member states that QMV represented an erosion of national sovereignty, there was nonetheless a genuine acceptance that its introduction was essential so as to ensure that individual member states could not block the future progress of the Community. As such, QMV was applied to a majority of the single market legislation, with only a few issues, such as the harmonisation of direct taxes, being excluded (primarily because of the insistence of Britain).

THE ROAD TO 1992

As part of an attempt to demonstrate the likely economic benefits of the single market, in 1986 and 1987 the Commission funded a project led by Paolo Cecchini to examine the 'costs on non-Europe' to demonstrate what the costs to the Community would be if the Community were to maintain a fragmented market. Making use of data from the four largest EC states, the Cecchini Report set out the costs to firms of maintaining customs controls and the opportunity costs of lost trade (Cecchini *et al.*, 1988). The Cecchini Report noted that significant economic benefits would accrue to the Community as the remaining barriers to the free movement of goods, capital, labour and services were removed. Specifically the EC could increase its GNP by 6.5 per cent if frontier and custom controls were removed and therefore economies of scale realised. Thus the gap between the Community and the US and Japan would be narrowed. The benefits would essentially come from four sources, namely cost savings for producers who would benefit from large-scale production; the so-called 'X' efficiency gains from enhanced managerial practices; the removal of technical barriers such as those restricting market entry or competition between the member states of the Community; and finally, the removal of physical barriers to trade such as border delays. The latter issue influenced the creation of the Schengen agreement on 14 June 1985 whereby West Germany, France and the Benelux countries agreed to the gradual abolition of frontier controls between them.

But despite these benefits, the implementation of the single market programme was not as quick as many would have liked. One of the problems that arose concerned the claims of the poorer member states (Greece, Ireland, Portugal and Spain) which advocated that, in return for their support for market liberalisation, the Community should provide greater spending on regional and social policy. In response to this situation, the Commission proposed a number of measures which aimed to close the gap between the Community's rich and poor member states (as well as between the rich and poor regions within the member states) by means of establishing a cohesion policy. Its effectiveness rested on the ability to secure a significant increase in the Community budget. Put another way, the richer member states of northern Europe would have to make greater financial contributions to the Community. Britain reacted negatively to this prospect of increasing the Community's budget and France and Germany were unwilling to direct existing Community resources to the poorer member states. One possible solution was to reduce the amount of spending on the common agricultural policy – which accounted for in excess of 50 per cent of the Community budget – as a means of solving the question of cohesion funding. But it was impossible to reach agreement. France and Germany were conscious that any reduction in the substantial subsidies that their farming communities received would have grim electoral consequences. The only option for solving the question of cohesion funding was thus to increase the Community budget. Yet because of the differences between Britain and the rest of the member states no progress was made on this issue throughout 1987 and it therefore appeared that, just as the budget had dominated the Community's agenda at the start of the 1980s, so too it would dominate the agenda at the end of the decade. The prospect of the Community once again becoming bogged down in the minutiae of budget negotiations instead of advancing towards the goal of creating a single market greatly concerned the German government, which agreed at the Brussels summit of February 1988 to pay the cohesion bill. Chancellor Kohl's decision to accept the burden of the financing of the cohesion policy ensured that the Community was able to proceed with the single market programme that had been set out in the SEA.

Not only did the SEA establish the objective of a single market, it also raised the question of Economic and Monetary Union in two paragraphs of the Preamble and Article 20 of the text. Among the 12 Community member states, France and Germany (to a lesser extent) were supportive of the objective of monetary union, arguing (among other reasons) that it would benefit the EC's competitiveness. This viewpoint had been considerably influenced by a 1987 report which argued that national control over monetary policy and the presence of national exchange rates did not sit with the objectives of free trade and capital mobility that had been set out in the single market programme (Padoa-Schioppa, 1987). France was additionally attracted to the idea of EMU because it offered it an opportunity to exercise influence over European financial policy which had hitherto been dominated by Germany and the German Deutschmark.

Among the other member states, the British Prime Minister Margaret Thatcher was by far the most vociferous in her opposition to the goal of EMU and the deeper forms of integration that Delors advocated. In her view, it was unacceptable for European integration to encroach on fundamental aspects of national sovereignty, such as social and monetary policy. She regarded the internal market programme as the pinnacle of European integration and not as the launchpad for further initiatives, with these beliefs being reflected in her famous speech at the College of Europe in Bruges in September 1988 [*Doc.33*]. Yet these views did not have total support within her government as many senior Cabinet ministers argued that it was impossible to just ignore the fact that the majority of other member states were supportive of the deepening of European integration. This included the belief that a genuine single market could only ever be achieved by creating a single currency, as the presence of distinct national currencies was a hindrance to the Community's economic development. The argument here was that the moves to establish the single market created a series of 'spillover' effects that impacted on other areas of the Community and reinforced the neo-functionalist viewpoint that greater economic and political integration was not wholly dependent on the member states.

A growing consensus among member states about the need to investigate the possibility of EMU resulted in the decision being taken at the June 1988 Hanover European Council to create a committee to examine the means by which monetary union would be established. The Committee, which was to be chaired by Jacques Delors, was charged with presenting its proposals so that they could be examined at the June 1989 Madrid European Council. When the Committee published its findings in April 1989, it recommended a three-stage transition to monetary union: first, the completion of the single market; second, the coordination of national monetary policies through a European System of Central Banks; and finally, the irrevocable locking of exchange rates and the transfer of monetary authority to a European Central Bank (ECB) [*Doc.34*]. Reaction among the member states to the Delors Report on EMU was, with the exception of Britain, generally positive, buoyed by the success of the Exchange Rate Mechanism in stabilising currency fluctuations among the participating member states. Apart from these internal factors, the decision of member states to agree at the Strasbourg European Council of December 1989 to establish an intergovernmental conference on EMU as a means of setting a formal path towards the creation of a single currency was influenced by the external events that were marked by the fall of the Berlin wall on 11 November 1989 and the subsequent break-up of the Soviet-controlled governments in Central and Eastern Europe in 1990. In addition to its influence in motivating states to progress towards monetary union, the geo-political changes ensured that the Community's focus quickly shifted towards political as well as economic issues.

CHAPTER SIX

THE TRANSFORMATION OF EUROPE: 1990–2004

By the end of the 1980s the EC had emerged from the sluggish progress that had affected its development from the mid-1960s until the early 1980s. A change in the Community's fortunes had been influenced by internal and external factors. This included the 1985 appointment of the dynamic Jacques Delors as President of the European Commission and awareness among member states and institutional actors of the need to improve economic growth rates within the Community because of the strong competition provided by Japan and the United States. The single market programme that emerged from this environment prompted an examination of areas of integration that had hitherto rested with member state governments. This included the question of monetary union and the establishment of common policies dealing with social affairs. For many member states, the logic behind these initiatives was self-evident: the establishment of a single market would lead to calls for the creation of a single currency and the need for uniform social standards to avoid companies 'chasing' cheaper labour costs in those member states which had lower levels of social provision. The latter had been influenced by the accession of Portugal and Spain in 1986 that resulted in a further widening of the levels of social policy provision within the Community.

The proposed deepening of cooperation on social affairs was not shared by all member states. Greece, Portugal and Spain were concerned about the costs involved in implementing new social standards and argued that their agreement to deepen the EC's competence in this area would be dependent on the receipt of additional financial support from the Community. Britain was particularly unwilling to accede to the view that the Community should expand its remit into social policy. It was a view that had been shaped by the changes that successive Conservative governments had imposed on the British economy since 1979, which had resulted in a deregulation of industrial practices that the government argued assisted with an improvement in Britain's economic competitiveness. The British government was therefore opposed to any development within the field of social policy on both economic and political grounds and stressed that decisions relating to social and monetary policy (among others) should be taken at the national level. Prime Minister Thatcher 'considered it quite inappropriate for rules and regulation about working practices or welfare benefits to be set at the Community level' (Thatcher, 1993: 750). Such debates over the scope and remit of the Community's competence were a key feature of the 1990s, being influenced by the desire of many member states to accelerate the process of European integration and the need for the Community to respond to the changed geopolitical European landscape as a result of the break-up of the Soviet-sponsored regimes in Central and Eastern Europe.

EUROPE'S CHANGING MAP

The European landscape in the postwar period had been influenced by the bipolar division of Europe along East–West lines and shaped by the institutions that underpinned this division. For Western Europe this took the form of NATO and the EC, while for Eastern Europe it took the form of the Warsaw Treaty Organisation and the founding of the Council for Mutual Economic Assistance (Comecon). Although the superpower influence of the United States and the Soviet Union had been crucial in underpinning these institutions, the 1985 election of Mikhail Gorbachev as General Secretary of the Soviet Union resulted in a change in policy that was emphasised by the introduction of *glasnost* (openness), *perestroika* (restructuring) and *novye myshlenye* (new thinking). Central to Gorbachev's reforms was the pursuit of domestic priorities – particularly economic growth – and the jettisoning of expensive foreign policy commitments. The latter included the need to engage in a drastic reduction in defence expenditure as the Soviet Union could no longer maintain a 'balance of power' with the United States and this in turn resulted in a series of superpower summits that led to a 1987 agreement to destroy intermediate-range missiles.

Although Moscow's changed foreign policy priorities were initially marked by a withdrawal from the third world, it in turn led to a loosening in the Soviet grip on the countries of Central and Eastern Europe. This culminated in Gorbachev's announcement at a Warsaw Pact meeting in the summer of 1989 that 'each people determines the future of its own country. There must be no interference from outside'. The implication of this was clear: the Soviet Union would not use force to suppress protests against the Communist governments of Central and Eastern Europe. The reality of Gorbachev's message directly resulted in the unelected and unpopular Communist governments being replaced with pro-Western administrations. Poland was the first country to go down the road of reform, marked by the Solidarity labour organisation transforming itself into a political party and its leader, Lech Walesa, becoming President. Elsewhere, the barbed-wire barriers to the West were removed in Hungary (resulting in thousands of people entering Western Europe), Erich

Honecker's East German regime was toppled in November 1989 along with the Berlin Wall that graphically illustrated the East–West division, while Communist governments in Czechoslovakia and Bulgaria were also overthrown. The whole process took place without bloodshed – with the exception of Romania, where nearly 1,000 people died. This instalment of democratic governments from Czechoslovakia to Poland was referred to as the 'Velvet Revolution' by the Czech playwright and dissident, Vaclav Havel.

These events redrew the geographical and institutional map of Europe. The Warsaw Treaty Organisation became defunct in early 1991 and the Soviet army retreated home from their bases in Central and Eastern Europe. But while Gorbachev's willingness to permit freedom for the Central and Eastern European satellites marked an end to the cold war conflict, he was less willing to allow freedom within the 15 republics that comprised the Soviet Union, fearing that this would lead to a break-up of the Soviet Union and an end to the influence of the Communist Party which had ruled since the 1917 revolution. Claims for independence from Moscow nevertheless materialised, particularly from the Baltic states of Estonia, Latvia and Lithuania that had been annexed by Stalin in 1940. Faced with an overwhelming support in the Baltic states for total independence from the Soviet Union, Moscow eventually acceded to their wish, while Gorbachev's resignation in December 1991 (after the August 1991 coup) marked the downfall of the Soviet Union as it split into its separate republics.

Nowhere more so was this changed landscape apparent than in the case of Germany, which after having been divided into East and West Germany was formally unified in October 1990. Yet the prospect of unification and the emergence of an even stronger Germany at the heart of Europe alarmed a number of European leaders. This was particularly true for Britain and France. At the same time, the United States was concerned that the EC might become insular and pursue its own interests at a time when the threat of Communism was no longer strong enough to hold the NATO alliance together. In other words it would lessen US influence on European affairs. This changed landscape raised questions over the role of the organisations that had defined the cold war, in particular NATO and the EC (and to a lesser extent the Western European Union). At the heart of this debate lay two competing visions. First, a 'Europeanist' view that was principally propagated by France, Germany, Belgium and Spain, which emphasised the need for a stronger European Community to include some form of defence identity through the WEU and by consequence a lessening of the reliance on the United States and NATO. Second, an 'Atlanticist' view that was advanced by Britain, Denmark, Portugal and the Netherlands which, despite acknowledging the need for a stronger EC, nevertheless stressed that NATO should remain the primary vehicle for Europe's defence and that a strong link should be maintained with the US.

Faced with this changed security environment, NATO began to stress its potential as a peacekeeping and humanitarian body in the post-cold war era and at the same time developed close relations with the former members of the Warsaw Treaty Organization through the new forum of the North Atlantic Co-operation Council. By 1994, the reality of Europe's new security environment had resulted in the former Warsaw Treaty Organization members developing even closer relations with NATO through the Partnership for Peace (PfP) programme. Such close relations would lead to Russian forces being deployed in 1996 as part of a NATO-led Implementation Force (IFOR) to secure peace following the civil war in Bosnia-Herzegovina, while a NATO–Russia Council was established in 2002 to provide closer cooperation and respond to common threats such as the struggle against terrorism. At the same time, NATO's membership expanded in 1999 to include the Czech Republic, Hungary and Poland. Parallel to this change in NATO's security remit, US concern about the possible destabilisation of the transatlantic relationship led to the November 1990 Transatlantic Declaration. It aimed to assuage concerns on both sides of the Atlantic over any weakening in transatlantic relations by providing a more formal set of links between the US and Europe, which were further reinforced by the 1995 New Transatlantic Agenda [*Doc.41*]. Moreover, it was reflective of an overarching US strategy in the post-1945 era to support European integration on the one hand but on the other to develop methods by which European integration could be contained within an Atlantic framework.

In a climate of change, EC member states were themselves attempting to map out the future development of the Community. Having established a timetable for the creation of a single market, the President of the European Commission, Jacques Delors, turned the Commission's attention in the late 1980s to achieving the goals of Economic and Monetary Union and social policy integration and in so doing emphasised the Commission's role as a 'policy entrepreneur'. Progress towards EMU demonstrated both a convergence of member state interests and at the same time the spillover effects from the European Monetary System, the single market programme and capital movement liberalisation. A combination of French support and German compliance resulted in a decision being taken at the June 1988 Hanover European Council to establish a committee of experts – under Delors' chairmanship – to examine how monetary union might be achieved. The 'Delors Committee' presented a report in April 1989 which detailed a three-stage route to currency union: the completion of the single market; the coordination of national monetary policies through a European System of Central Banks; and the irrevocable locking of exchange rates and the transfer of monetary authority to a European Central Bank [*Doc.34*]. At the Strasbourg European Council of December 1989 member states took the decision to convene an IGC on EMU before the end of 1990. The Strasbourg meeting was also noticeable for producing an agreement on a Social Charter (without British support) and for discussing the prospect of German reunification.

The dramatic nature of these events influenced the decision of French President François Mitterrand and German Chancellor Helmut Kohl to issue a joint letter on 19 April 1990. It stressed that an IGC on European Political Union should be convened because of the 'far reaching changes in Europe' and the need to 'define and implement a common foreign and security policy' [*Doc.35*]. Apart from defining a foreign and security policy, they sought to strengthen the Community's democratic legitimacy and improve the effectiveness of the EC's institutions. Just as Britain had been against the holding of an IGC on EMU, it was also against the further political development of the Community. The British government did not share the Franco–German argument that an IGC on political union was necessary to deal with the challenges posed by the collapse of Communism and German unity. The British position was moreover reflective of a broader preference for EC reform to take place via quiet developments rather than by means of high-profile treaty negotiations. In British eyes the Community was already overburdened by the need to complete the single market and the impending EMU negotiations. Yet this was a view that was not shared by the other member states, which took a majority decision at the June 1990 Dublin European Council to convene a second IGC that would focus on European political union.

THE MAASTRICHT TREATY

At the Maastricht European Council of December 1991 the heads of government of the member states concluded the work of the IGC negotiations on monetary union and political union that had commenced 12 months before at the December 1990 Rome European Council. Of the two IGCs, the negotiations on monetary union were by far the most straightforward and benefited from them having been subject to detailed reports and analysis prior to the commencement of the talks, and having been conducted by a relatively small group of people, comprising national Treasury ministers and officials and central bank representatives. The political union negotiations were far from straightforward. This was influenced by the fact that little preparatory work had been undertaken prior to the commencement of the talks and because of the range of topics that they covered. Discussions on political union primarily concentrated on strengthening the role of the European Parliament, establishing a European citizenship, the development of new common policies such as culture and interior affairs, the improvement of existing policies including social policy and the environment, and the creation of a common foreign and security policy.

The array of topics that the political union negotiations embraced highlighted the extent to which the Community had changed since its foundations in the 1957 Treaty of Rome. The creation of policies dealing with interior affairs had been prompted by an acknowledgement of the need to tackle common problems such as drug trafficking and illegal immigration through the creation of new forms of cooperation at the EC level. National ministries had traditionally controlled a number of the policies that the IGC dealt with, including those on interior affairs, and as such the IGC negotiations impacted on areas of government that had by custom rested with member states. One consequence of this process was to increase the number of national government ministries that were directly affected by the political union negotiations, which ranged from social affairs to the environment. The significance of these developments was fourfold. First, the range of topics and number of people involved increased the complexity of the talks. Second, it highlighted a decline in the role of the national foreign ministry to control and shape a member state's European policy. Third, the expansion in the Community's reach of influence pointed to a Europeanisation of national government which was reflective of the impact that European integration had on policy-making within the member states. Fourth, it pointed to a strengthening of the regulatory function played by the Commission and signalled in certain policy areas, such as the environment, a strengthening of the Commission's negotiating role on external policy matters.

The scope of topics covered by the political union negotiations led to considerable differences of views among the member states as to the nature of the proposals. This particularly applied to Britain, despite Prime Minister John Major's commitment to be 'at the heart of Europe'. Britain's vision of European integration thus continued to be significantly different from that of most of the other member states, with the government being unwilling to support moves to deepen European political integration. Such a stance was fuelled by traditional British concerns over the loss of national sovereignty and the need for Prime Minister Major to keep the Conservative Party united by placating Eurosceptic members of the government. The British government was particularly concerned about proposed references to the creation of a 'federal' Europe and the development of a European social policy; it believed the latter would reduce labour market flexibility and lessen the competitiveness of the economy. Britain was additionally unwilling to be tied into a commitment to accept the single currency and argued that any initiatives in the area of foreign and security policy – including the strengthening of the Western European Union – should not disentangle the United States from Europe or undermine the role of NATO as Europe's security guarantor. The latter point was also shared by Denmark, the Netherlands and Portugal. In the case of Britain, such a conclusion had been informed by the reality of the Gulf War, which suggested that a separate European security and defence identity was unlikely to emerge, not least because Britain had been one of the few EC member states that had played (and was able to play) a significant role in the 1991 Gulf conflict.

Britain's unwillingness to accept certain policies, and the need for the Treaty to be agreed by the common accord of all member states, ensured that in classic EU fashion the final Treaty design was riddled with compromises. Greece, Portugal and Spain demanded extra financial assistance for their support for cooperation on social and monetary integration. France demanded that a deadline be set for the start of the single currency. Germany was particularly eager to ensure that a future monetary union did not include countries with a weak currency, on the basis that it could lead to instability in the system as a whole. Germany therefore advocated the need for economic convergence to precede monetary union and that any EMU text should include such priorities as low inflation. The outcome of the December 1991 Maastricht European Council was a Treaty on European Union which confirmed that member states (or rather national governments) were firmly in control of the integration process. The Treaty established a three-stage route to monetary union and confirmed that a single currency would begin no later than 1 January 1999. The irrevocability of this decision led the British government to insist on the insertion of a special Protocol to the treaty that would allow it to opt out from the single currency. The route that was chosen for EMU broadly reflected previous recommendations that included a first stage (1990–93) of strict budgetary discipline. Stage two, which commenced on 1 January 1994, was primarily concerned with the establishment of a European Monetary Institute that would strengthen the level of coordination between member states. This included the need for national governments to adhere to strict requirements relating to public spending and price stability. In this context, the emphasis attached to sound economic policies meant that the single currency project would help to ensure that member states pursued stable economic policies, thereby being somewhat reflective of Alan Milward's thesis that the process of European integration had been central to the 'rescue of the nation state' (Milward, 1992).

For a member state to be eligible to proceed to the third stage of EMU – and thereby participate in the single currency – it would have to satisfy four convergence criteria [*Doc.36*]. These were an average rate of inflation of not more than 1.5 per cent higher than that of the three best-performing member states; a budget deficit of not more than 3 per cent of gross domestic product and a public debt ratio not to exceed 60 per cent of GDP; participation in the 2.25 per cent narrow bands of the ERM for two years without severe tension or devaluation; and an interest rate which during the previous year should not have been more than 2 per cent higher than that of the three best-performing member states. The European Council would take the decision over which states had met the convergence criteria, and although the Treaty included a provision that EMU could start in 1997 if a majority of member states had met the criteria, this proved to be impossible because of a difficult economic climate. In 1996 only Ireland and Italy were certain to meet the convergence criteria, while Italy's public debt of 124 per cent of GDP ensured that it was way off the target. Concerned about the economic costs of the single currency commitment, the less-developed member states of Greece, Ireland, Portugal and Spain secured additional financial support via the creation of a cohesion fund that was designed to assist environmental and infrastructure projects in those countries to ensure that they met the convergence criteria requirements of the single currency.

In contrast to the finality of the monetary union negotiations to establish a single currency, the political union negotiations produced a series of compromise agreements that failed to reflect all the interests of the most pro-integrationist member states. Britain's unwillingness to support the aim of a 'federal goal' ensured that the final treaty made reference to the EU as 'a new stage in the process of creating an ever closer union among the peoples of Europe'. British intransigence extended to the question of social policy, where the government's unwillingness to accept the setting of social policy legislation at the Community level resulted in a separate Social Protocol being secured outside of the Treaty. This in effect meant that the social policy measures agreed to by the other 11 member states would be implemented by intergovernmental cooperation rather than by EC law. But while such an outcome pleased the British government, the decision would not stop the Commission from initiating legislation that was applicable to all member states under the health and safety provisions that had been introduced in the Single European Act, thereby resulting in John Major's government subsequently challenging the introduction of regulations on working hours.

Elsewhere, the Treaty continued the practice established in the SEA of widening the number of policy areas covered by qualified majority voting. The Treaty also extended the Community's competences in more than a dozen areas. This included the acceptance of the notion of European citizenship and the extension of the Community's powers in the areas of consumer protection, culture, education, environment, health, industry, research and technological development, social policy and vocational training. Agreement was also reached on the establishment of a common foreign and security policy (CFSP) that was a compromise between the Franco–German 'Europeanist' vision and the British-led preference for the maintenance of the 'Atlanticist' link. Thus, while the agreement allowed for the establishment of common positions and joint actions on foreign policy, the WEU was kept separate from the EC and NATO's remit as Europe's security guarantor was confirmed [*Doc.37*]. Decisions on CFSP and justice and home affairs were moreover set with an intergovernmental 'pillar' framework and as such the supranational impact of the Community did not extend to these policies. This outcome favoured the views of those member states which wanted to ensure that national governments would remain the key decision-makers on foreign policy and judicial cooperation.

To account for this intergovernmental method of cooperation, the institutional arrangements of the Community were based on a new pillar structure. The first pillar comprised the EC and contained common policies and actions that involved the supranational institutions of the Community. This included the European Parliament, which was given the right to approve (or not) the European Commission, while a new co-decision procedure with the Council ensured that the European Parliament would be able to block or amend EC legislation by majority vote. This therefore ensured that the European Parliament could 'no longer be accused of lacking teeth'. An enhancement of the European Parliament's influence necessitated the European Commission and member states reassessing their approach to policy-making, which had hitherto essentially bypassed the European Parliament. Thus, because the European Parliament was given the ability to block legislation via the co-decision procedure, both the European Commission and the member states had to pay greater attention to the views of the Parliament in the legislative process. Other changes that the Treaty introduced included the establishment of a new Committee of the Regions and the insertion of the subsidiarity provision which stressed that decisions should be taken closest to the citizen at the lowest level of institutional authority. Pillars two and three dealt with CFSP and justice and home affairs (JHA) respectively, with cooperation taking place on an intergovernmental basis and not involving the Community's supranational institutions, while the European Union encompassed all of these elements.

Although the Maastricht Treaty was signed in February 1992, it did not formally enter into force until 1 November 1993. The delay was caused by difficulties over its ratification by the member state governments which had been significantly influenced by Denmark's rejection of the Treaty in a referendum in June 1992 by 50.7 to 49.3 per cent, or some 42,000 votes. The Danes, who had wanted to be the first to ratify the Treaty, consequently sparked a ratification crisis that was followed by the French electorate accepting the Treaty by the slimmest of margins in September 2002: 51.05 to 48.95 per cent. And while the Treaty was in the end passed in a second referendum in Denmark in May 1993, albeit only after its government obtained an opt-out on defence policy and a further clarification of its opt-out from the single currency, the whole process weakened the level of confidence in the EU's future development. Increasing scepticism about the stability of the EU's fortunes was not helped by a crisis in the Exchange Rate Mechanism from July 1992 until August 1993, during which time Britain and Italy were forced to leave the system. These events lessened the support for the EU among an electorate that concluded the Maastricht Treaty to be 'a Treaty too far' and this in turn impacted on the scope and success of future treaty reform.

ENLARGING THE EU

A reduction in the support for the EU within the member states and a hardening in Euroscepticism did not deter non-EU countries from seeking membership. The opposite was the case. The changing nature of European integration in the late 1980s and early 1990s had brought a number of European Free Trade Association countries to conclude that they were disadvantaged through being outside of the then EC. The response of the Community was in the first instance to propose the creation of a new form of EC–EFTA association as a means of preventing an immediate enlargement at a time when the Community's energies were focused on the single market programme. To this end, a 1992 EC–EFTA agreement was signed to create a European Economic Area (EEA) that was intended to lead to full EU membership. The EEA, which came into existence in January 1994, was designed to provide for the free movement of capital, goods, services and workers.

Far from forestalling an immediate EU enlargement, the EEA negotiations spurred on the desire of Austria, Finland, Norway and Sweden to join the Union. (Switzerland had initially shown a willingness to join the EU, but dropped its application in the wake of a negative 1992 EEA vote.) As with previous enlargements, the negotiations were focused on those policy areas that were most sensitive to national interests. For Austria, Finland and Sweden, this included the question of whether their neutrality would hinder their ability to participate in the EU's CFSP that included a commitment to the 'eventual framing of a common defence'. But it proved to be a relatively uncontroversial issue, with the Austrian, Finnish and Swedish governments being prepared to accept the CFSP in a post-cold war environment. More controversial issues included the question of EU environment policy, as standards were for the most part higher in the applicant countries. Other troublesome questions included energy and fisheries policy, primarily as a result of Norway's refusal to surrender control to the EU. Disputes over these and other issues were nevertheless resolved and the four applicants signed treaties of accession in January 2004 that would in turn have to be ratified at the national level. But as Norway had held a referendum in November 1994 in which 52 per cent of the country's voters had decided against membership, only Austria, Finland and Sweden joined the EU on 1 January 1995.

Although the 1995 'northern' enlargement had been an uncomplicated process – all three countries were net contributors to the EU budget, had experience of intergovernmental cooperation in EFTA and had the necessary administrative and judicial structures to implement policies in the form of the *acquis communitaire* – it brought to the fore questions relating to the institutional design and the policies embraced by the EU. This was particularly relevant because of the prospect of future enlargement to Central and Eastern European states. Applications for membership had already been received from Cyprus, Malta and Turkey, when in June 1993 the Copenhagen European Council offered the prospect of membership to the countries of Central and Eastern Europe if the applicants were able to 'assume the obligations of membership by satisfying the economic and political conditions required'. For this to happen, the Council set out the exact tests that the applicants would have to pass for them to join the EU, the so-called 'Copenhagen criteria' [*Doc.38*]. As a result of the Copenhagen decision, applications for EU membership were received from Hungary and Poland in 1994; Bulgaria, Estonia, Latvia, Lithuania, Romania and the Slovak Republic in 1995; and the Czech Republic and Slovenia in 1996. These applications had been aided by the support that had been provided to them since the collapse of Communism, most notably in the form of 'Europe Agreements' which enabled them to participate in the economic, political and trading aspects of European integration.

Whereas the 1995 enlargement did not result in a wholesale reassessment of the institutional design of the EU, it was clear that the accession of more countries could not simply follow the practice of working within the parameters of existing institutional structures. In 1995, the College of Commissioners had simply increased in size from 17 to 20 to accommodate the three new members. Reform of the Commission – including the practice whereby the larger member states had two Commissioners – would therefore be a necessity prior to any future enlargement so as to avoid it becoming an unwieldy body. At the same time there was a need to extend the use of QMV – to avoid policies being blocked by the use of the national veto – and the need to examine the distribution of votes in the Council of Ministers. Outside these questions of institutional reform, the prospect of future enlargement motivated member states to discuss other issues. This included the prospect of large-scale migration from the accession countries, the reform of the common agricultural policy and the cohesion and structural funds which together accounted for approximately 80 per cent of the EU budget. Of these issues, the unwillingness of some member states (particularly France) to decrease the financial burden of the CAP had in the past limited the opportunity for reform, with the CAP continuing to account for approximately 50 per cent of the Community budget in the early 1990s. The prospect of EU enlargement to include countries with large agricultural sectors, which accounted for approximately 20 per cent of employment in Central and Eastern Europe (four times the EU level), meant that there was a need to reassess the principle of subsidising farmers on the basis of production and guaranteed prices. Pressure to reform the CAP was also influenced by the external climate of criticism in World Trade Organization talks that EU support for its farmers was an anti-competitive practice.

Such viewpoints influenced the Commission to propose in 1997 as part of its enlargement plans (Agenda 2000) to decouple the support for farmers from production and to link support to social and environmental objectives. But France refused to accept this proposal and as a consequence the scope of the reforms was severely limited. Thus, even though member states understood the implications that enlargement would have on the EU's institutions and policy areas, there was nevertheless reluctance by existing member states to fundamentally alter the 'cost–benefit balance sheet'. This was not least because of domestic political pressures that were compounded by the difficult economic conditions of the early 1990s, whereby unemployment in the existing 12 member states reached 17 million by early 1994. This difficult economic situation was made worse by governments having to make unpopular cuts in public expenditure to ensure that they met the convergence criteria requirements of the single currency [*Doc.36*].

TREATY OF AMSTERDAM

Member states were mindful of questions relating to institutional reform when they took the decision at the June 1994 Corfu European Council to convene a Reflection Group, under the chairmanship of the Spanish Diplomat Carlos Westendorp, to make preparations for the holding of yet another IGC. Despite the Treaty of Maastricht having come into force only on 1 November 1993, there was a commitment in Article N of that treaty to hold another IGC before the end of 1996. The Commission, Council and European Parliament were entrusted with the task of drawing up reports that would guide the work of the Reflection Group. The reports, which were presented in early 1995, emphasised a number of common themes. These included the effectiveness of the decision-making procedures, particularly with regard to the two intergovernmental pillars. Other themes were the need for greater openness, legitimacy, transparency and the simplification of procedures.

In focusing on these issues, the reports were mindful of the institutional implications that would result from further EU enlargement. A number of member states also welcomed the opportunity to review the extent of the effectiveness of the Maastricht reforms. This particularly applied to the CFSP, whereby the reality of the EU's experience in the former Yugoslavia had pointed to a number of shortcomings in the effectiveness of EU cooperation. A number of member states – chiefly Belgium, France, Germany, Italy, Luxembourg and the Netherlands – consequently viewed the IGC negotiations as an important opportunity to deepen European integration. This was, however, an assessment that was not shared by Denmark and Britain, both of which had been badly scarred by the crisis surrounding the ratification of the Maastricht Treaty. In Britain, this had assisted the cause of the Eurosceptic wing of the Conservative Party, which in turn limited the ability of the government to orchestrate a positive European policy. British hostility was therefore a common feature of the IGC negotiations which had commenced in March 1996, and it was only the election of the Labour government in May 1997 that created the possibility for the negotiations to conclude at the June 1997 Amsterdam European Council.

The product of the IGC negotiations was a Treaty of Amsterdam that made a number of minor amendments to the EU, but which lacked the sense of possessing a 'grand theme' (as the Maastricht Treaty had). The question of institutional reform – to prepare the EU to meet the challenge of enlargement – was largely avoided: the Treaty failed to tackle key issues such as the size of the Commission and the reweighting of a member state's votes in the Council of Ministers. The Treaty did, nevertheless, extend the scope of QMV to an additional 16 policy areas, while it also enhanced the role of the European Parliament by extending the co-decision procedure to embrace existing policies and new areas of responsibility. The effect of this was to ensure that the co-decision procedure would apply to more than 80 per cent of Council decisions. The Parliament was also given the power to confirm or refuse a nominated Commission President, with this augmentation in the Parliament's influence over the Commission being illustrated with the resignation of the Santer Commission in March 1999.

Concern over the ability of an enlarged EU to progress at a common pace resulted in the insertion of a number of flexibility clauses in the Treaty that would enable some countries to progress at a quicker pace of integration than others, albeit with the provision that member states would be able to block decisions in the Council as to whether flexibility should be used. Other notable changes included the incorporation of the Social Protocol into the EU proper (which John Major had opposed at the Maastricht European Council), being made possible by election of the British Labour government in May 1997. Improvements were also made to the CFSP as a result of European embarrassment to orchestrate a coordinated and effective response to the crises in the Balkans. Efforts were therefore made in the Treaty of Amsterdam to strengthen the cohesiveness of the CFSP through the appointment of a High Representative (to be combined with the post of Secretary-General of the Council). This effort to strengthen the EU's nascent foreign policy also resulted in a decision to create a policy-planning unit to advise the High Representative.

One of the most significant areas of change concerned the agreement to establish an area of freedom, security and justice, and resulted in a number of aspects of the justice and home affair provisions of the third pillar being incorporated in the regular first pillar provisions of the EU. This specifically applied to those matters that related to the free movement of people, including matters relating to asylum, immigration and visas. The Schengen agreement on the free movement of persons between member states was also incorporated into the first pillar provision of the EU. The effect of these changes was that the third pillar was renamed 'Police and Judicial Cooperation in

Criminal Matters'. This emphasis on the need for common action in police and judicial cooperation among member states was the product of the growing threats posed to member states from organised crime, including illegal immigration and money laundering. Terrorist threats were additionally an important factor, particularly in the wake of the 11 September 2001 attacks on the United States.

Overall, the Treaty of Amsterdam therefore produced a series of reforms that reflected incremental rather than whole-scale change. Improved cooperation on justice and home affairs and the extension of the co-decision procedure has to be set against the failure of the Treaty to fully prepare the EU for enlargement. Questions relating to the composition of the European Commission and the weighting of votes in the Council, which were central to the future enlargement plans, were avoided. Member states were also unable to agree on a reduction in the number of policy areas in which they maintained a right of veto. A lack of consensus among member states on a number of core issues ensured that the negotiations produced a Treaty that represented the lowest common denominator position where agreement could be produced among the member states. The reality of this need to achieve agreement over and above all else consequently led the member states to postpone the more complex issues for a future IGC, with the Treaty containing a Protocol which required that a further IGC be convened to carry out a review of the institutional provisions at least one year before EU membership exceeded 20 member states.

Beyond the parameters of the Amsterdam negotiations, member states achieved progress in the course of 1998 to further develop the capabilities of the CFSP with a view to the creation of a European Security and Defence Policy (ESDP), with this being influenced by the EU's inability to respond sufficiently quickly to the Kosovo crisis. Movement in this policy area had been aided by the convergence of the views of Britain (Atlanticist) and France (Europeanist) which led to a meeting in St Malo on 4 December 1998. The meeting produced a Letter of Intent on defence cooperation and a joint declaration on European defence in which both countries emphasised that while NATO would retain the main security responsibility for Europe, European member states would nevertheless increase their institutional arrangements for collaborative action in those areas that did not necessitate US involvement, such as peacekeeping. This agreement provided towards the decision taken at the December 1999 Helsinki European Council to create an ESDP based on the establishment of a multinational corps of 50,000 to 60,000 forces by 2003, with the capability of mounting an autonomous European mission if NATO declined to get involved in a crisis situation. Apart from progress on CFSP/ESDP matters, member states also made headway on the single currency. Here it was noticeable that whereas British input had been crucial to the CFSP/ESDP discussions, the government in London nevertheless continued to remain adrift from monetary union. Thus, the single currency came into existence in January 1999 as a result of 11 member states having met the convergence criteria requirements. Greece would later meet the criteria in January 2001 and as a result only Denmark, Sweden and Britain remained outside of the single currency when the changeover to the use of euro banknotes and coins commenced in January 2002.

TREATY OF NICE

Even though the Treaty of Amsterdam contained a Protocol commitment to carry out a further examination of EU reform, member states had concluded the necessity of institutional reform throughout 1998 and came to an agreement at the June 1999 Cologne European Council (only a month after the Treaty of Amsterdam came into force) to hold an IGC in 2000 that would address the issues that had been irresolvable at Amsterdam. The key issues included the size and composition of the Commission, the weighting of votes in the Council and the possibility of extending the use of qualified majority voting in the Council. The decision to hold yet another IGC negotiation had been influenced by the decision in 1999 to widen the accession negotiations to include all 13 countries (Bulgaria, Cyprus, Czech Republic, Estonia, Hungary, Latvia, Lithuania, Malta, Poland, Romania, the Slovak Republic, Slovenia and Turkey). This was instead of limiting the discussions to the six countries which had been engaged in accession talks since December 1997 (Cyprus, the Czech Republic, Estonia, Hungary, Poland and Slovenia). The opening up of the accession negotiations to all 13 countries consequently increased the likelihood of a large-scale enlargement which therefore added further urgency to the need to address the institutional questions which the Treaty of Amsterdam had been unable to resolve.

The IGC negotiations commenced in February 2000 under the presidency of Portugal with a limited agenda that reflected the desire of the member states to focus specifically on the institutional matters that had been left over from the Treaty of Amsterdam so as to prepare the EU for enlargement. By the time of the June 2000 Feira European Council, the IGC agenda had been widened to include the question of 'closer cooperation', by which member states would be able to cooperate more closely with other member states in individual areas. A widening of the IGC did not, however, suggest that differences between the member states on institutional matters had been resolved. A divergence of views was particularly apparent at the October 2000 Biarritz European Council (which was the last meeting of heads of state and government before the December Nice summit). Key areas of divergence included the future shape of the European Commission, whereby the larger member states' suggestion of a smaller Commission based on a rotation system was criticised by the smaller member states.

A lack of consensus between member states continued to the December 2000 Nice European Council, with agreement on a new treaty that provided the green light for enlargement being achieved only after four days of negotiations. The lengthy nature of these negotiations reflected the desire of member states to achieve some form of agreement rather than no agreement. Discussions over institutional reform were among the most problematic. These included the questions of QMV and the reform of the Commission. Although most member states were aware of the need for greater use of QMV in an enlarged EU, some governments nevertheless wanted to ensure that certain policies would continue to be governed by the national veto. Britain stressed that defence, social security and taxation could not be subject to QMV. Ireland and Luxembourg shared Britain's concerns about taxation, while Germany was unwilling to extend QMV to asylum and immigration policy. As befitting its status as one of the main benefactors of EU funding, Spain obtained an agreement that the use of the national veto would continue until 2007 for any agreements to provide financial assistance to poorer countries. In the end, the Treaty of Nice, which was signed on 26 February 2001 and came into force on 1 February 2003, resulted in an agreement to extend QMV to nearly 40 additional treaty provisions, while the number of votes distributed among the member states was altered to take account of the EU's increased population [*Doc.39*]. It was, however, not a whole-scale adjustment of votes, as small states continued to be over-represented and Germany's status as having the largest population did not transcend into more votes. This was primarily because of French concern about allowing Germany to have more votes than the other large member states. The QMV agreement was also extremely complex, comprising three elements: first, the support of in excess of 70 per cent of the member states' weighted votes; second, the support of a majority of the member states; and finally, the necessity that those states in favour of the decision comprised not just 70 per cent of the weighted votes but also represented at least 62 per cent of the EU population.

In terms of the size and composition of the Commission, it was apparent that existing arrangements whereby the number of Commissioners simply increased with each enlargement would in the end produce an unwieldy body. This was because, when compared with the six countries that signed the Treaty of Rome, the EU's membership would have increased four-fold with the accession of ten additional member states. In practical terms, the EU would comprise too many countries for it to work in an effective manner based on existing methods of decision-making. For this reason there was a need to revise the practice whereby the largest member states of Britain, France, Germany, Italy and Spain had two Commissioners and the remaining member states one Commissioner. In the end, agreement was reached at Nice that from 1 January 2005 there would be one Commissioner per member state, thereby resulting in the five largest member states having to give up their right to have two Commissioners. It was also agreed that the total number of Commissioners would in future not exceed 26 members and therefore if the EU were to grow to more than 27 members, the total number of Commissioners would be less than the number of member states. So as to ensure that all members would be treated fairly in an EU of 27 or more member states, the Treaty introduced a commitment to a principle of a rotation system. The treaty also provided for a redistribution of votes in the European Parliament, which both set a total limit of 732 MEPs (the Amsterdam Treaty had set a ceiling of 700 MEPs) and sought to provide a more equitable distribution of seats among the member states [*Doc.39*]. The treaty also extended the application of the co-decision procedure to seven treaty articles, including judicial cooperation in civil matters (apart from family law).

THE FIFTH ENLARGEMENT AND CONSTITUTIONAL REFORM

Notwithstanding the fact that the exclusive focus of the Treaty of Nice on institutional matters ensured that its remit was not as wide as that of the SEA, Maastricht or Amsterdam Treaties, member states acknowledged that the final Treaty did not provide an optimal outcome. As such, a Declaration was annexed which stressed that yet another IGC would be convened to examine the institutional arrangements necessary for enlargement. To fully discuss these issues, at the December 2001 Laeken European Council, member states adopted the Laeken declaration on the Future of Europe which identified the need for the EU to improve its internal workings and to ensure that it was capable of playing a full and active role in world affairs. The latter point had been further clarified by the September 2001 terrorist attacks on the US. In terms of the enlargement negotiations, the Laeken meeting also noted that negotiations with ten applicant states – namely Cyprus, Estonia, Hungary, Latvia, Lithuania, Malta, Poland, the Slovak Republic, the Czech Republic and Slovenia – should be concluded by the end of 2002. (It is expected that Bulgaria and Romania will join by 2007, while at the time of writing Turkey is not negotiating its membership.) To further examine the issues that were raised at Laeken, member states took a decision to convene a Convention that would undertake the preparatory work for the IGC.

The Convention, which was chaired by former French President Valéry Giscard d'Estaing, met between March 2002 and June 2003 and discussed a number of proposals that reflected a desire to improve the quality of leadership offered by the EU, streamline its institutional structures and ensure that its range of policies reflected the challenges that the EU faced. Such points were set out in a series of recommendations that were presented in the form of a draft Constitutional Treaty in June 2003 and which in turn served as the basis for the IGC negotiations that commenced a few months later, in October, and concluded at the Brussels summit of 18 June 2004. By that time the European Union had enlarged to 25 member states with the accession of Cyprus, Estonia, Hungary, Latvia, Lithuania, Malta, Poland, the Slovak Republic, the Czech Republic and Slovenia on 1 May 2004 and in so doing increased the EU population by more than 100 million people.

The final outcome of the IGC negotiations was agreement at the Brussels European Council of June 2004 on a new Constitutional Treaty that consolidated all the previous treaties into one single document to provide the EU with a simpler and more accessible set of rules. This effort to add clarity to the EU and improve many of its procedures had led some observers to incorrectly conclude that the Treaty was merely a 'tidying up' exercise. Instead, the Treaty makes a number of important reforms that aim to improve the EU's ability to respond to the challenges posed by enlargement. One of the most difficult issues to resolve in the negotiations concerned the system of majority voting in the Council of Ministers that had been agreed to in the Treaty of Nice. Criticism of the Nice agreement rested on two arguments: first, that the three-stage QMV procedure was far too complex; second, that the distribution of votes was unfair. Thus, Germany and other member states argued that it was unjust to provide Poland and Spain with nearly as many votes as the larger EU countries [*Doc.39*]. For Germany this was a particularly important argument. It posed the legitimate question as to why it should have only a few more votes than member states which not only had approximately half of its population but which made either no or merely minimal contributions to the EU budget while Germany's financial contribution accounted for between 25 and 30 per cent of the total EU budget.

Having increased their influence in the Nice Treaty, Poland and Spain were predictably unwilling to contemplate a change to a system that favoured their interests. The upshot of this was that it proved impossible to broker a suitable agreement at the Brussels summit of December 2003. This state of affairs would continue until the election of a new Spanish government in March 2004 that brought with it a stronger willingness to resolve Spain's differences in the discussions over the Constitutional Treaty. As a result, member states reached agreement in June 2004 on a new simplified 'two-stage' procedure, whereby an agreement would be reached if it was supported by 55 per cent of the member states as long as this reflected 65 per cent of the EU population [*Doc.39*]. Such an outcome reinforced the influence of the larger member states that represented the majority of the EU population. In addition to altering the voting threshold, member states took the decision to extend majority voting to 44 new policy areas. This included the area of justice and home affairs that had previously been governed primarily by intergovernmental methods of decision-making. Such an initiative reflected the need for member states to work more effectively in their efforts to tackle matters relating to illegal migration, terrorism and cross-border crime. Nevertheless, concerns over the maintenance of national interest resulted in the introduction of a new 'emergency break' formula in some of the policy areas that are now subject to majority voting. The new procedure, which would be applied to social security and criminal procedural law, ensured that where a member state is in disagreement with a majority vote decision it is able to refer the matter back to the Council (at which stage the Council can either accept the proposal on a unanimity basis or ask the Commission for a new proposal).

One of the most significant developments concerned the creation of a post of EU President, to be elected by heads of government for a term of two-and-a-half years [*Doc.42*]. Such a change was prompted by concerns that the previous system of a six-monthly rotation of the President among all member states hindered the continuity of EU policies and created confusion for non-member states. Concern over the EU's international identity led to the creation of an EU Minister for Foreign Affairs that will combine the existing positions of the Council's High Representative for foreign policy and the European Commissioner for external relations [*Doc.42*]. In short, the new post will provide a single spokesperson who will be able to provide a clearer coordination of EU foreign policy, which ranges from diplomatic negotiations to the distribution of foreign aid. Linked to this issue of foreign policy, the Treaty strengthened EU defence policy by permitting a core group of countries to enhance their cooperation on military matters if such a move is approved in the Council by majority vote. Thus, those member states that are more willing (and more able) will take a stronger role in EU military operations [*Doc.37*]. A final notable change was the incorporation of the Charter of Fundamental Rights into the Treaty, thereby demonstrating the support of all member states to a range of rights that are applicable to EU citizens.

These latest changes have predictably raised Eurosceptic concerns about the erosion of national sovereignty and have given rise to claims that a new European superstate is in the making. In truth, such claims do not reflect the reality of the constitutional treaty. As I have stressed throughout this book, the changes that emerge from IGC negotiations and which in turn confer competences to the EU are the product of agreement among all member states. Thus, the first article of the Treaty states that 'this constitution establishes the European Union, on which member states confer competences to attain objectives they have in common. The Union shall coordinate the policies by which the member states aim to achieve these objectives, and shall exercise on a Community basis the competences they confer on it'. In short, the capabilities granted to the EU are those which member states have reached agreement on, with the remainder of competences resting with the member state governments. Thus, member states retain control of taxation policy and despite improvements in the capabilities of the EU to tackle JHA and CFSP matters, the EU does not possess a police force or an army. Enhancements in the EU's capability in external relations (such as the new EU Foreign Minister), the potential for some member states to advance cooperation on military matters and the move to majority voting on JHA are pragmatic and practical developments that reflect the challenges that EU member states must grapple with and, more importantly, highlight the need for cooperation to solve these problems.

Success in tackling these issues will depend on the actions of the member state governments and the leadership of the European Commission, which since November 2004 has comprised 25 Commissioners (one from each member state) and has been led by the relatively unknown former Portuguese Prime Minister, José Manuel Barroso. For the immediate future, member states still have the task of ratifying the new constitutional treaty for it to take effect. As experience has shown, this is not a simple process and is complicated by the fact that at least 9 out of the 25 member states are committed to hold referendums on the treaty.

PART THREE   ASSESSMENT

CHAPTER SEVEN

THE FUTURE OF EUROPEAN INTEGRATION

The European Union has changed dramatically over the last half century, having grown from 6 to 25 member states [*Doc.38*]. At the same time the institutional, decision-making and policy competences of the EU have altered since its foundation by the 1957 Treaty of Rome [*Doc.15*]. At a wider level the European continent of the 21st century is not as divided and does not suffer the same difficulties that beset much of the post-1945 period. The iron curtain that Winston Churchill described in March 1946 [*Doc.2*] has been replaced by a series of agreements that have brought the countries of Eastern Europe in from the cold and many of them have become members of the EU [*Doc.38*]. That is not to say that Europe is a continent that is at peace with itself. Trouble spots and tension remain, most recently in the Balkans where European nations have attempted to grapple with a succession of conflicts throughout the 1990s and into the 21st century. The institutions of the EU and its member states have also had to respond to a number of new problems that have replaced the concerns of the cold war. Today, so called 'low security' problems, such as crime, terrorism and migration, concern the minds of policy-makers.

The nature of the linkage between the EU and the member states has also been subject to a great deal of change. Back in 1965 the French President, Charles de Gaulle, withdrew his government's participation from the Council of Ministers and the Committee of Permanent Representatives in protest over plans by the European Commission to strengthen the powers of the European Parliament and develop the use of majority voting in the Council of Ministers. Commonly known as the 'empty chair crisis', de Gaulle's actions were motivated by a fear that the potential for majority voting would threaten French national interests. Thus, whereas de Gaulle was prepared to tolerate European integration when it favoured French interests, as in the area of agriculture, he resisted the encroachment of policies into areas that he considered to be the prerogative of national governments [*Doc.20*]. Two decades later, the British Prime Minister, Margaret Thatcher, equally demonstrated the importance of member states in the decision-making process by blocking the progress of the

then Community until Britain obtained a satisfactory rebate and renegotiation of its budget contributions [*Doc.30*]. President de Gaulle and Prime
Minister Thatcher shared a similar view that national governments should
remain the key decision-makers.

Today, it is apparent that national governments continue to hold a dominant position in the EU and the manner by which the EU has evolved has
primarily been a consequence of the decisions taken by the governments
rather than the EU institutions. Thus, while such factors as the end of the cold
war, the leadership capacity of the European Commission and the decisions of
the European Court of Justice have been influential in shaping the direction
of European integration, for all intents and purposes it has been the decisions
of the member state governments that have ultimately determined the path of
European integration. The expansion in the number of policies that the EU
embraces, from the relatively limited areas of coal and steel to matters relating
to the environment (bathing water standards) and key aspects of economic
policy (the single currency), has been shaped by the decisions taken by the
member states. Key treaty reforms, including the Single European Act and
the Maastricht Treaty on European Union, which enhanced the powers of
EU institutions (particularly the European Parliament), have also been the
product of the agreements of member state governments.

Many of these changes have been the result of necessity, whereby collaboration with other member states has been the only means by which it has
been possible to tackle key matters of public policy and to ensure a degree of
harmonisation of standards across all member states. To take an example, the
development of EU environmental policy was influenced by the reality that
environmental pollution extends beyond member state boundaries and as
a consequence individual member state government action to tackle such
problems would be futile. At the same time, member state governments with
strict environmental standards did not want the competitiveness of their
companies to be lessened by companies in other member states with inferior
standards charging lower prices. The harmonisation of environmental standards was therefore perceived to be the only way to resolve these problems,
while the creation of a coordinated policy would also permit the EU to have a
stronger influence in international environmental negotiations.

The EU's involvement in such a wide range of policies has been an
influential factor in shaping the views of those individuals who argue that
it would be better to solve problems at national and sub-national levels. In
response to such criticism, greater emphasis has been attached to the principle
of subsidiarity, which advocates the taking of decisions at the lowest possible
level, including the member state. Yet in the face of this criticism of EU
interference, it is nonetheless the case that the tackling of issues at the EU level
is in many instances the only possible option. Moreover, because of the
expansion in the number of member states and the increased potential for

competing views, it has also been necessary for more decisions to be taken on the basis of majority voting whereby an individual or group of member states can be outvoted. This change in decision-making has, however, occurred out of necessity: in an enlarged grouping of member states progress can really be achieved only through the use of majority voting so as to overcome the threat of a national veto [*Doc.39*].

And just as there has occurred a lack of distinction between domestic and EU policies, the role of the EU institutions has also changed. A question over the democratic basis of the EU has resulted in the European Parliament (whose members are directly elected) gaining greater influence in every treaty reform. The need to ensure that member states and companies conform to new European standards has seen a concurrent increase in the workload of the European Court of Justice, which has been called on to offer rulings on a whole range of topics, from working hours to the free movement of goods [*Doc.29*]. The necessity to establish commonality within the EU has, at the same time, required the European Commission to take an active role in 'policing' the implementation of directives and regulations which has, in turn, led to discussion over the extent to which the EU has become a 'regulatory state'.

Such points may lead to a conclusion that 'unity' is a significant feature of the European Union. However, it is also true that diversity is just as common. First, divisions exist between member states over the future direction that the EU should take and not all governments are participants in all EU policies. To take one example, on 1 January 2002, 12 out of a total of 15 EU member states started the process of replacing their distinct national currencies with euro banknotes and coins (Britain, Denmark and Sweden declined to participate) [*Doc.36*]. Second, EU legislation, such as that relating to the single market, is not implemented at the same speed in all member states [*Doc.32*]. Third, there are notable distinctions in the process, structure and conduct of the governance of member states. For instance, not all governments operate similar welfare state models, with the comprehensive approach provided by Scandinavian countries not being mirrored in the Mediterranean countries of Greece, Portugal and Spain. Fourth, there remain significant differences in the internal labour markets of EU member states, with some countries, such as Britain, being typified by a more flexible labour market with a higher proportion of part-time employees. The study of the EU therefore directs our attention to both the factors that promote unity and the identification of those points that illustrate continuing diversity.

Observers would be wrong to conclude that these are a weakness of the EU. Instead, the ability for groups of countries to work together on specific policies is an essential strength of the European integration process. It is clearly impossible for a grouping of at least 25 member states to reach agreement on every policy initiative. Each member state brings specific resources to the EU and moreover has particular interests that it wishes to advance. That is not to say that the future of European integration is likely to take the form of a two-speed Europe, whereby an identifiable group of countries will be reduced to the slow-lane. Rather, it is more likely that the future rests on some form of 'pick 'n' mix' approach that will result in member states engaging in specific policies that represent its interests. Thus, British absence from participation in the single currency and its reluctance to support any initiatives for the harmonisation of taxation policy would be counterbalanced by its ability and willingness to take a leading role in matters relating to defence policy. By contrast, other member states, such as Austria and Ireland, have traditionally refused to engage on defence matters but are likely to support initiatives such as the single currency. In short, the reinforcing of this flexibility in the constitutional treaty enhances the ability of the EU to respond to the challenges that it faces in the 21st century.

PART FOUR · DOCUMENTS

DOCUMENT 1   THE BRIAND MEMORANDUM, 1 MAY 1930

In this document, the French Foreign Minister, Aristide Briand, set out his aims for the organisation of a system of European Federal Union.

Compelled by their geographical position to live together, the peoples of Europe, if they are to enjoy security and prosperity, must establish a permanent regime of joint responsibility for the rational organization of Europe . . .

The entente between European nations must be realized on the plane of their absolute sovereignty and complete political independence. Moreover, it would be impossible to associate the idea of political domination with any organization which (like the present one) is deliberately placed under the control of the League of Nations . . .

. . . Never has the time been so propitious and so pressing for the beginning of constructive work in Europe. By the settlement of the principal moral and material problems arising out of the war Europe will soon be freed from heavy burdens, spiritual and economic. The new Europe will be ready for a positive effort, answering to the new order. It is the decisive hour for Europe to listen and choose her own fate. To unite, in order to live and prosper: that is the necessity which confronts European nations today. The peoples seem to have made their feelings clear. The governments must now accept their responsibilities. Otherwise the grouping of material and moral forces for the common benefit which it is their collective task to control will be abandoned to the dangers and chances of uncoordinated individual initiatives.

Leiden University Historical Institute website:
http://www.let.leidenuniv.nl/history/rtg/res1/briand.htm

DOCUMENT 2   WINSTON CHURCHILL'S SPEECH AT WESTMINSTER COLLEGE, FULTON, MISSOURI, 5 MARCH 1946

In this document Winston Churchill highlighted the growing threat of Communism and argued the need for non-Communist countries to unite and for a close association to develop between the United States and Britain.

From Stettin in the Baltic to Trieste in the Adriatic, an iron curtain has descended across the continent. Behind that line lie all the capitals of the ancient states of Central and Eastern Europe. Warsaw, Berlin, Prague, Vienna, Budapest, Belgrade, Bucharest and Sofia, all these famous cities and the populations around them lie in the Soviet sphere and all are subject in one form or another, not only to Soviet influence but to a very high and increasing measure of control from Moscow. Athens alone, with its immortal glories, is free to decide its future at an election under British, French and American observation . . .

. . . If the population of the English-speaking Commonwealths be added to that of the United States, with all that such cooperation implies in the air, on the sea and in science and industry, there will be no quivering, precarious balance of power to offer its temptation to ambition or adventure. On the contrary, there will be an overwhelming assurance of security.

Robert Rhodes James (ed.) (1974) *Winston S. Churchill: His Complete Speeches 1897–1963*, Vol.VII, 1943–49, (Langhorne: Chelsea House), pp.7285–93.

DOCUMENT 3   WINSTON CHURCHILL'S SPEECH AT ZURICH UNIVERSITY ON THE SUBJECT OF A UNITED STATES OF EUROPE, 19 SEPTEMBER 1946

In this extract, Churchill calls for an immediate start to be made to bringing European states closer together. Although some observers concluded that this demonstrated a wholehearted commitment to European unity by Britain, the underlying theme was that Britain would be 'with Europe' but not 'of Europe'.

And what is the plight to which Europe has been reduced? Some of the smaller States have indeed made a good recovery, but over wide areas a vast, quivering mass of tormented, hungry, care-worn and bewildered human beings gape at the ruins of their cities and homes, and scan the dark horizons for the approach of some new peril, tyranny or terror . . .

Yet all the while there is a remedy which, if it were generally and spontaneously adopted, would as if by miracle transform the whole scene and would in a few years make all Europe, or the greater part of it, as free and as happy as Switzerland is today. What is this sovereign remedy? It is to re-create the European family, or as much of it as we can, and provide it with a structure under which it can dwell in peace, in safety and in freedom. We must build a kind of United States of Europe . . .

. . . The first step in the re-creation of the European family must be a partnership between France and Germany. In this way only can France recover the moral leadership of Europe. There can be no revival of Europe without a spiritually great France and spiritually great Germany. The structure of the United States of Europe, if well and truly built, will be such as to make the material strength of a single state less important. Small nations will count as much as large ones and gain their honour by their contribution to the common cause . . .

. . . In all this urgent work, France and Germany must take the lead together. Great Britain, the British Commonwealth of Nations, mighty America and

I trust Soviet Russia – for then indeed all would be well – must be the friends and sponsors of the new Europe and must champion its right to live and shine.

Randolph S. Churchill (ed.) (1948) *The Sinews of Peace. Post-War Speeches by Winston S. Churchill* (London: Cassell), pp.198–202

DOCUMENT 4 **THE MARSHALL PLAN. SPEECH BY THE US SECRETARY OF STATE GENERAL GEORGE MARSHALL AT HARVARD UNIVERSITY, 5 JUNE 1947**

The Marshall Plan provided the framework for over $13 billion of financial assistance from the United States.

. . . The truth of the matter is that Europe's requirements for the next three or four years of foreign food and other essential products – principally from America – are so much greater than her present ability to pay that she must have substantial additional help or face economic, social and political deterioration of a very grave character . . .

. . . It is logical that the United States should do whatever it is able to do to assist in the return of normal economic health in the world, without which there can be no political stability and no assured peace. Our policy is not directed against any country or doctrine but against hunger, poverty, desperation and chaos. Its purpose should be the revival of a working economy in the world so as to permit the emergence of political and social conditions in which free institutions can exist . . .

Department of State Bulletin, 15 June 1947, pp.1159–60

DOCUMENT 5 **THE BEVIN SPEECH ON WESTERN UNION. EXTRACT FROM AN ADDRESS BY BRITISH FOREIGN SECRETARY ERNEST BEVIN, HOUSE OF COMMONS, 22 JANUARY 1948**

This document demonstrates the desire of the British government to find a suitable post-war foreign policy. Despite this attempt to engage Britain in the construction of Europe, British policy-makers considered that the nation's position was best served by close association with the US and not through being involved in a new power base. Bevin soon lost his enthusiasm for a 'Western Union' and the Labour government boycotted the May 1948 Hague Congress which advocated the creation of a European Assembly.

It must be recognised that the Soviet Government has formed a solid political and economic block behind a line running from the Baltic along the Oder, through Trieste to the Black Sea . . .

I believe therefore that we should seek to form with the backing of the Americans and the Dominions a Western democratic system comprising, if possible, Scandinavia, the Low Countries, France, Portugal, Italy and Greece . . . I believe therefore that the moment is ripe for a consolidation of Western Europe. This need not take the shape of a formal alliance, though we have an alliance with France and may conclude one with other countries. It does, however, mean close consultation with each of the Western European countries, beginning with economic questions. We in Britain can no longer stand outside Europe and insist that our problems and position are quite separate from those of our European neighbours . . .

Provided we can organise a Western European system such as I have outlined above, backed by the power and resources of the Commonwealth and of the Americas, it should be possible to develop our own power and influence to equal that of the United States and the USSR. We have the material resources in the Colonial Empire, if we develop them, and by giving a spiritual lead now we should be able to carry out our task in a way which will show clearly that we are not subservient to the United States of America or to the Soviet Union.

'The first aim of British foreign policy', Cabinet Memorandum by the Secretary of State for
Foreign Affairs, Ernest Bevin, 4 January 1948, CAB 129/23, Public Record Office

DOCUMENT 6   TREATY OF ECONOMIC, SOCIAL AND CULTURAL
COLLABORATION AND COLLECTIVE SELF-DEFENCE
BETWEEN THE UNITED KINGDOM OF GREAT
BRITAIN AND NORTHERN IRELAND, BELGIUM,
FRANCE, LUXEMBOURG AND THE NETHERLANDS
(THE BRUSSELS TREATY), BRUSSELS,
17 MARCH 1948

The Brussels Treaty committed Britain, France and the Benelux countries to a common defence system and to strengthen their relationship with each other so that they would be able to overcome threats to their security, including those of an ideological, political or military nature.

Article IV
If any of the High Contracting Parties should be the object of an armed attack in Europe, the other High Contracting Parties will, in accordance with the provisions of Article 51 of the Charter of the United Nations, afford the Party so attacked all the military and other aid and assistance in their power.

http://www.nato.int/docu/basictxt/b480317a.htm

DOCUMENT 7   THE NORTH ATLANTIC TREATY, WASHINGTON DC, 4 APRIL 1949

This document is an extract from the Treaty of Washington. A desire to establish a common defence system had been set out in the 1948 Brussels Treaty, although the start of the Berlin blockade in the summer of 1948 accelerated the momentum towards widening the security and defence relations of the Brussels Treaty. The Treaty entered into force in August 1949, with the commitment to collective defence being embodied in Article 5.

Article 5

The Parties agree that an armed attack against one or more of them in Europe or North America shall be considered an attack against them all and consequently they agree that, if such an attack occurs, each of them, in exercise of the right of individual or collective self-defence recognised by Article 51 of the Charter of the United Nations, will assist the Party or Parties so attacked by taking forthwith, individually and in concert with the other Parties, such action as it deems necessary, including the use of armed force, to restore and maintain the security of the North Atlantic area.

http://www.nato.int/docu/basictxt/treaty.htm

DOCUMENT 8   THE STATUTE OF THE COUNCIL OF EUROPE, 5 MAY 1949

The Council of Europe was established on an intergovernmental principle for the purpose of building peace.

Article 1

(a) The aim of the Council of Europe is to achieve a greater unity between its Members for the purpose of safeguarding and realising the ideals and principles which are their common heritage and facilitating their economic and social progress.

(b) This aim shall be pursued through the organs of the Council by discussion of questions of common concern and by agreements and common action in economic, social, cultural, scientific, legal and administrative matters and in the maintenance and further realisation of human rights and fundamental freedoms.

(c) Participation in the Council of Europe shall not affect the collaboration of its members in the work of the United Nations and of other international organisations or unions to which they are parties.

(d) Matters relating to national defence do not fall within the scope of the Council of Europe.

http://conventions.coe.int/treaty/en/Treaties/Html/001.htm

DOCUMENT 9   **THE SCHUMAN DECLARATION. STATEMENT BY THE FRENCH FOREIGN MINISTER ROBERT SCHUMAN ON POOLING THE PRODUCTION OF COAL AND STEEL IN EUROPE, PARIS, 9 MAY 1950**

Robert Schuman's plan provided the basis for the establishment of the European Coal and Steel Community (ECSC). The British government was opposed to the proposal on the grounds that British coal and steel production was significantly greater than that of other European countries and because of an unwillingness to entrust authority to a supranational body.

The French Government proposes that Franco-German production of coal and steel be placed under a common 'high authority', within an organisation open to the participation of the other European nations.

The pooling of coal and steel production will immediately ensure the establishment of common bases for economic development as a first step in the federation of Europe, and will change the destinies of those regions which have long been devoted to the manufacture of arms, to which they themselves were the constant victims.

The common production thus established will make it plain that any war between France and Germany becomes not only unthinkable but materially impossible. The establishment of this powerful entity, open to all countries willing to take part, and eventually capable of making available on equal terms the fundamental elements of industrial production, will give a real foundation to their economic unification . . .

By pooling basic production and by creating a new high authority whose decisions will be binding on France, Germany and the other countries that may subsequently join, these proposals will lay the first concrete foundation for a European Federation which is so indispensable to the preservation of peace . . .

http://europa.eu.int/abc/symbols/9-may/decl_en.htm

DOCUMENT 10   **THE PLEVEN PLAN. STATEMENT BY THE FRENCH PRIME MINISTER, RENÉ PLEVEN, AT THE FRENCH NATIONAL ASSEMBLY ON THE CREATION OF A EUROPEAN ARMY, 24 OCTOBER 1950**

The Pleven Plan's proposal for a European Defence Community (EDC) created some controversy because it noted that a rearmed Germany could contribute units to a defence force, albeit one that was under a unified supranational command. Four years later the French National Assembly rejected the EDC Treaty.

The creation of a European Army cannot result from a simple joining up of national military units. This would in reality only conceal a coalition of the old type. For tasks which are inevitably common ones, only common institutions will do. The army of a united Europe, composed of men coming from different European countries, must bring about, as near as possible, a complete fusion of its human and material components under a single political and military authority . . .

This European army would be financed from a common budget. The European minister of defence would be responsible for the implementation of existing international obligations and for the negotiation and implementation of new international engagements on the basis of directives received from the council of ministers. The European armament and equipment programme would be laid down and implemented under his authority.

The participating states which currently have national forces at their disposal would retain their own authority over that part of their existing forces which was not integrated into the European army . . .

It is on the basis I have just sketched out that the French Government proposes to invite Great Britain and the free countries of continental Europe, should they agreed to participate in the creation of a European army, to work together on ways of realising the principles just explicated. Those studies would begin in Paris as soon as the coal and steel treaty is signed . . .

Official Journal, Debates, 25 October 1950, no.104 (pp.7118–19) translated

DOCUMENT 11 **TREATY ESTABLISHING THE EUROPEAN COAL AND STEEL COMMUNITY, PARIS, 18 APRIL 1951 (TREATY OF PARIS)**

The Treaty of Paris signified the first crucial step on the path to European economic and political integration. When the European Coal and Steel Community (ECSC) came into existence in June 1952 it established the first supranational institution which had been influenced by the Schuman Plan proposal of 9 May 1950.

Preamble
THE PRESIDENT OF THE FEDERAL REPUBLIC OF GERMANY, HIS ROYAL HIGHNESS THE PRINCE ROYAL OF BELGIUM, THE PRESIDENT OF THE FRENCH REPUBLIC, THE PRESIDENT OF THE ITALIAN REPUBLIC, HER ROYAL HIGHNESS THE GRAND DUCHESS OF LUXEMBOURG, HER MAJESTY THE QUEEN OF THE NETHERLANDS,

CONSIDERING that world peace can be safeguarded only by creative efforts commensurate with the dangers that threaten it,

CONVINCED that the contribution which an organised and vital Europe can make to civilisation is indispensable to the maintenance of peaceful relations,

RECOGNISING that Europe can be built only through practical achievements which will first of all create real solidarity, and through the establishment of common bases for economic development,

ANXIOUS to help, by expanding their basic production, to raise the standard of living and further the works of peace,

RESOLVED to substitute for age-old rivalries the merging of their essential interests; to create, by establishing an economic community, the basis for a broader and deeper community among peoples long divided by bloody conflicts; and to lay the foundations for institutions which will give direction to a destiny henceforward shared,

HAVE DECIDED to create a European Coal and Steel Community . . .

http://europa.eu.int/abc/obj/treaties/en/entr30a.htm#11

DOCUMENT 12   **THE EUROPEAN DEFENCE COMMUNITY TREATY, PARIS, 27 MAY 1952**

The European Defence Community Treaty was an ambitious plan that sought to establish a defence commitment at a time when no progress had been made in establishing the political institutional framework that such a commitment would require. A response to the 1954 French rejection of the Treaty was the creation of the Western European Union.

Article 1
The High Contracting Parties, by the Present Treaty, set up among themselves a European Defence Community, supranational in character, comprising common institutions, common Armed Forces, and a common budget.

Article 2

1. The objectives of the Community are exclusively defensive.
2. Consequently, under the conditions set forth in this Treaty, it shall ensure the security of member states against any aggression by taking part in Western defence within the framework of the North Atlantic Treaty; by integrating the defence forces of the member states; and by the rational and economical employment of their resources.
3. Any armed attack against any of the member states in Europe or against the Europe Defence Forces shall be considered an armed attack on all member states.

   The member states and the European Defence Forces shall afford to the State or forces so attacked all the military aid in their power.

DOCUMENT 13 PROTOCOL MODIFYING AND COMPLETING THE BRUSSELS TREATY (WESTERN EUROPEAN UNION), PARIS, 23 OCTOBER 1954

In the wake of the French rejection of the EDC Treaty, Britain proposed that the 1948 Brussels Treaty should be modified to allow Germany and Italy to become members. As a result the Brussels Treaty was transformed into the Western European Union, comprising in 1954 seven members: Belgium, France, Germany, Italy, Luxembourg, the Netherlands and the UK.

Article I
The Federal Republic of Germany and the Italian Republic hereby accede to the Treaty as modified and completed by the present Protocol.

The High Contracting Parties to the present Protocol consider the Protocol on Forces of Western European Union (hereinafter referred to as Protocol No. II), the Protocol on the Control of the Armaments and its Annexes (hereinafter referred to as Protocol No. III), and the Protocol on the Agency of Western European Union for the control of Armaments (hereinafter referred to as Protocol No. IV) to be an integral part of the present Protocol.

Article II
The sub-paragraph of the Preamble to the Treaty: 'to take such steps as may be held necessary in the event of renewal by Germany of a policy of aggression' shall be modified to read: 'to promote the unity and to encourage the progressive integration of Europe.'

The opening words of the second paragraph of Article I shall read: 'The co-operation provided for in the preceding paragraph, which will be effected through the Council referred to in Article VIII . . .'

Article III
The High Contracting Parties will make every effort in common to lead their peoples towards a better understanding of the principles which form the basis of their common civilisation and to promote cultural exchanges by conventions between themselves or by other means.

http://www.nato.int/docu/basictxt/b541023g.htm

DOCUMENT 14 THE MESSINA DECLARATION. RESOLUTION ADOPTED BY THE MINISTERS OF FOREIGN AFFAIRS OF THE MEMBER STATES OF THE ECSC, MESSINA, 1–2 JUNE 1955

This document is an extract from the declaration by the foreign ministers of the Six in June 1955 that reflected the desire of their governments to advance European integration. The Messina conference established an intergovernmental committee under the chairmanship of Paul-Henri Spaak, the report of which provided the basis for the two Treaties establishing the European Economic Community (EEC) and the European Atomic Energy Community (Euratom).

The Governments of the Federal Republic of Germany, Belgium, France, Italy, Luxembourg and the Netherlands believe the time has come to make a fresh advance towards the building of Europe. They are of the opinion that this must be achieved, first of all, in the economic field.

They consider that it is necessary to work for the establishment of a united Europe by the development of common institutions, the progressive fusion of national economies, the creation of a common market and the progressive harmonisation of their social policies.

I

To these ends, the six Ministers have agreed on the following objectives:

A. 1. The expansion of trade and the freedom of movement call for the joint development of the major channels of communication.

  A joint study will accordingly be undertaken of development plans based on the establishment of a European network of canals, motor highways, electrified railways, and on a standardisation of equipment, as well as a study of possible means of achieving a better coordination of air transport . . .

2. The development of atomic energy for peaceful purposes will in the near future open up the prospect of a new industrial revolution out of all proportion to that which has taken place over the last hundred years. The six signatory States consider that it is necessary to study the creation of a common organisation to be entrusted with the responsibility and the means for ensuring the peaceful development of atomic energy, while taking into account the special arrangements made by certain Governments with third countries . . .

B. The six governments recognise that the establishment of a European market, free from all customs duties and all quantitative restrictions, is the objective of their action in the field of economic policy . . .

C. The creation of a European Investment Fund will be studied. The objective of this fund would be the joint development of European economic potentialities and in particular the development of the less developed regions of the participating states.

D. As regards the social field, the six governments consider it essential to study the progressive harmonisation of the regulations in force in the different countries, notably those which concern working hours, overtime rates (night work, Sunday work and public holidays) and the length and rates of pay for holidays . . .

S. Patijn (ed.) (1970) *Landmarks in European Unity: 22 Texts on European Integration* (Leiden: A.W. Sijthoff), pp.93–9

DOCUMENT 15   **THE TREATY OF ROME ESTABLISHING THE EUROPEAN ECONOMIC COMMUNITY, ROME, 25 MARCH 1957**

The EEC Treaty set out the main principles of the common market, established a customs union and a common external tariff, as well as a range of other Community policies, such as agriculture, transport and competition.

Article 2
The Community shall have as its aim, by establishing a common market and progressively approximating the economic policies of member states, to promote throughout the Community a harmonious development of economic activities, a continuous and balanced expansion, an increase in stability, an accelerated raising of the standard of living and closer relations between its member states.

Article 3
For the purposes set out in Article 2, the activities of the Community shall include, as provided in this Treaty and in accordance with the timetable set out therein:

(a) the elimination, as between member states, of customs duties and of quantitative restrictions on the import and export of goods, and of all other measures having equivalent effect;
(b) the establishment of a common customs tariff and of a common commercial policy towards third countries;
(c) the abolition, as between member states, of obstacles to freedom of movement for persons, services and capital;
(d) the adoption of a common agricultural policy;
(e) the adoption of a common transport policy;
(f) the establishment of a system ensuring that competition in the common market is not distorted;
(g) the application of procedures by which the economic policies of member states can be coordinated and disequilibria in their balances of payments remedied;

(h) the approximation of the laws of member states to the extent required for the proper functioning of the common market;
(i) the creation of a European Social Fund in order to improve employment opportunities for workers and to contribute to the raising of their standard of living;
(j) the establishment of a European Investment Bank to facilitate the economic expansion of the Community by opening up fresh resources;
(k) the association of the overseas countries and territories in order to increase trade and to promote economic and social development.

Article 9

1   The Community shall be based upon a customs union which shall cover all trade in goods and which shall involve the prohibition between member states of customs duties on imports and exports and of all charges having equivalent effect, and the adoption of a common customs tariff in their relations with third countries . . .

Article 38

1   The common market shall extend to agriculture and trade in agricultural products . . .
4   The operation and development of the common market for agricultural products must be accompanied by the establishment of a common agricultural policy among the member states.

Article 48

1   Freedom of movement for workers shall be secured within the Community by the end of the transitional period at the latest.

Article 92

1   Save as otherwise provided in this Treaty, any aid granted by a Member State or through State resources in any form whatsoever which distorts or threatens to distort competition by favouring certain enterprises or the production of certain goods shall, insofar as it affects trade between member states, be incompatible with the common market . . .

Article 237

Any European State may apply to become a member of the Community. It shall address its application to the Council, which shall act unanimously after consulting the Commission . . .

http://europa.eu.int/abc/obj/treaties/en/entoc05.htm

DOCUMENT 16   **BRITAIN'S FIRST APPLICATION FOR EEC MEMBERSHIP**

In these documents the British government set out a series of conditions that had to be met if it was to enter the Community (a), and in so doing marked a shift in focus away from the Commonwealth and Empire towards Europe (b).

(a)

. . . No British Government could join the European Economic Community without prior negotiation with a view to meeting the needs of the Commonwealth countries, of our European Free Trade Association partners, and of British agriculture . . .

During the past nine months, we have had useful and frank discussions with the European Economic Community Governments. We have now reached the stage where we cannot make further progress without entering into formal negotiations . . .

Therefore, after long and earnest consideration, Her Majesty's Government have come to the conclusion that it would be right for Britain to make a formal application under Article 237 of the Treaty negotiations with a view to joining the Community if satisfactory arrangements can be made to meet the special needs of the United Kingdom, of the Commonwealth and of the European Free Trade Association . . .

> Extracted from statement by Harold Macmillan on the first British application
> to the European Economic Community, *Parliamentary Debates* (Hansard),
> House of Commons, Fifth Series, Vol.645, pp.928–31

(b)

The decision of Harold Macmillan's government to apply for membership of the European Community represented an historic moment in post-war politics. It determined the direction not just of British policy, but also that of Europe and the Atlantic alliance . . . It signalled the end of a glorious era, that of the British Empire, and the beginning of a whole new chapter of British history. The 'three circles' concept, to which Anthony Eden devoted his speech at the Conservative Party conference at Margate in 1953, and which had been the mainstay of British foreign policy since the war, was no longer valid. Eden described Britain then as being at the centre of three circles: the United States, the Commonwealth and Europe. Theoretically, this gave Britain an all-powerful position in world affairs. In actual fact, even by that time this was no longer justifiable. The United States became increasingly engrossed in its non-violent contest with the other superpower. As more and more of the colonies became independent they pursued their own policies, particularly in trade and other economic affairs, and Britain was less able to influence them in their general policies . . .

Edward Heath (1998) *The Course of My Life* (London: Hodder & Stoughton), p.203

DOCUMENT 17   **FRANCE'S REJECTION OF BRITISH EEC MEMBERSHIP. PRESS STATEMENT BY FRENCH PRESIDENT CHARLES DE GAULLE, 14 JANUARY 1963**

This document reproduces an extract of General de Gaulle's speech which cast a veto against Britain's first application for EEC membership. A combination of Britain's reliance on the US for defence and an insistence on satisfying a list of preferences prior to membership provided de Gaulle with sufficient grounds to veto the British application.

. . . England is, in effect, insular, maritime, linked through its trade, markets, and food supply to very diverse and often very distant countries. Its activities are essentially industrial and commercial, and only slightly agricultural. It has, throughout its work, very marked and original customs and traditions. In short, the nature, structure, and economic context of England differ profoundly from those of the other States of the Continent . . .

It must be agreed that first the entry of Great Britain and then that of those other States will completely change the series of adjustments, agreements, compensations, and regulations already established between the Six, because all these States, like Britain, have very important traits of their own. We would then have to envisage the construction of another Common Market. But the 11-member, then 13-member, and the perhaps 18-member Common Market that would be built would, without doubt, hardly resemble the one the Six have built.

Moreover, this Community, growing in that way, would be confronted with all the problems of its economic relations with a crowd of other States, and first of all with the United States.

It is foreseeable that the cohesion of all its members, who would be very numerous and very diverse, would not hold for long and that in the end there would appear a colossal Atlantic Community dependent on the US and under American leadership which would soon completely swallow up the European Community.

Charles de Gaulle (1970) *Discours et Messages, Pour l'effort Août 1962 – Décembre 1965* (Paris: Librairie Plon) pp.66–70 (translated)

THE FRANCO–GERMAN TREATY OF FRIENDSHIP, PARIS, 22 JANUARY 1963

This document represents the cornerstone of the cooperation that has taken place between France and Germany in the postwar years. The Franco–German Treaty focuses on three main areas: the holding of regular summits and meetings of foreign ministers, cooperation within the realm of defence and security (which was for many years of a limited nature) and education.

I ORGANISATION

1. The Heads of State and Government shall issue as and when necessary the requisite directives and shall regularly follow the implementation of the programme specified below. They shall meet as often as may be necessary and in principle at least twice a year.

II PROGRAMME

A. *Foreign Affairs*

1. The two Governments shall consult each other, prior to any decision, on all important questions of foreign policy, and particularly on questions of mutual interest, with a view to achieving as far as possible an analogous position. Such consultations shall cover, *inter alia*, the following subjects:

- Problems concerning the European communities and European political cooperation;
- East–West relations, in both the political and the economic fields;
- Matters dealt with in the North Atlantic Treaty Organisation and the various international organisations which are of interest to the two Governments, particularly in the Council of Europe, the Western European Union, the Organisation for Economic Cooperation and Development, the United Nations and its specialised agencies.

1963: A Retrospective of the Political Year in Europe
(Paris: WEU Assembly, 1964)

DOCUMENT 19 **THE MERGER TREATY. TREATY ESTABLISHING A SINGLE COUNCIL AND A SINGLE COMMISSION OF THE EUROPEAN COMMUNITIES, BRUSSELS, 8 APRIL 1965**

This document comes from the Merger Treaty that established joint institutions for the European Atomic Energy Community, the European Coal and Steel Community and the European Economic Community. The Treaty came into force on 1 July 1967. The desire to establish a common Council of Ministers and a Commission that served all three Communities was regarded as an essential step towards European integration.

THE COUNCIL OF THE EUROPEAN COMMUNITIES

Article 1
A Council of the European Communities (hereinafter called the 'Council') is hereby established. This Council shall take the place of the Special Council of Ministers of the European Coal and Steel Community, the Council of the European Economic Community and the Council of the Atomic Energy Community.

It shall exercise the powers and jurisdiction conferred on those institutions in accordance with the provisions of the Treaties establishing the European Coal and Steel Community, the European Economic Community and the European Atomic Energy Community, and of this Treaty.

THE COMMISSION OF THE EUROPEAN COMMUNITIES

Article 9
A Commission of the European Communities (hereinafter called the 'Commission') is hereby established. The Commission shall take the place of the High Authority of the European Coal and Steel Community, the Commission of the European Economic Community and the Commission of the European Atomic Energy Community.

It shall exercise the powers and the jurisdiction on those institutions in accordance with the provisions of the Treaties establishing the European Coal and Steel Community, the European Economic Community and the European Atomic Energy Community, and of this Treaty.

http://europa.eu.int/abc/obj/treaties/en/entoc112.htm

DOCUMENT 20   **THE LUXEMBOURG COMPROMISE. AGREEMENT ON DECISION-MAKING REACHED AT THE EXTRAORDINARY SESSION OF THE LUXEMBOURG EEC COUNCIL, 28–29 JANUARY 1966**

This document is an extract from the Luxembourg Compromise which resolved the 1965 empty chair crisis.

Majority voting procedure

I.   Where, in the case of decisions which may be taken by a majority vote on a proposal of the Commission, very important interests of one or more partners are at stake, the Members of the Council will endeavour, within a reasonable time, to reach solutions which can be adopted by all the Members of the Council while respecting their mutual interests and those of the Community, in accordance with Article 2 of the Treaty.

II.   With regard to the preceding paragraph, the French delegation considers that where very important interests are at stake the discussion must be continued until unanimous agreement is reached.

III. The six delegations note that there is a divergence of views on what should be done in the event of a failure to reach complete agreement.

IV.   The six delegations nevertheless consider that this divergence does not prevent the Community's work being resumed in accordance with the normal procedure.

Bulletin of the European Economic Community, 1966, No.3, pp.8–9

DOCUMENT 21   **BRITAIN'S SECOND APPLICATION FOR EEC MEMBERSHIP. STATEMENT BY BRITISH PRIME MINISTER HAROLD WILSON ON THE SECOND APPLICATION FOR MEMBERSHIP OF THE EUROPEAN ECONOMIC COMMUNITY, HOUSE OF COMMONS, LONDON, 2 MAY 1967**

The second British application reflected a general feeling that another failure could not be risked, not least because Britain's economic fortunes had continued to decline throughout the 1960s.

First, there are the problems associated with the operation of the common agricultural policy of the Community – the problems of its potential effects on the cost of living and on the structure and well-being of British agriculture; problems of the budgetary and balance of payments implications of its system of financing; and certain Commonwealth problems with which I will deal in a moment . . .

There are also highly important Commonwealth interests, mainly in the field of agriculture, for which it is our duty to seek safeguards in the negotiations. These include, in particular, the special problems of New Zealand and of Commonwealth sugar-producing countries, whose needs are at present safeguarded by the Commonwealth Sugar Agreement . . .

We do not see European unity as something narrow or inward-looking. Britain has her own vital links through the Commonwealth, and in other ways, with other continents. So have other European countries. Together we can ensure that Europe plays in world affairs the part which the Europe of today is not at present playing. For a Europe that fails to put forward its full economic strength will never have the political influence which I believe it could and should exert within the United Nations, within the Western Alliance, and as a means for effecting a lasting détente between East and West; and equally contributing in ever fuller measure to the solution of the world's North–South problem, to the needs of the developing world.

Parliamentary Debates (Hansard), House of Commons, Fifth Series,

Vol.746, pp.310–14

DOCUMENT 22   **THE HAGUE SUMMIT. FINAL COMMUNIQUE OF THE MEETING OF HEADS OF STATE AND GOVERNMENT OF THE EC COUNTRIES, THE HAGUE, 2 DECEMBER 1969**

The Hague summit had the triple objective of completion, consolidation and enlargement of the communities. Two important reports emanated from the meeting, one on monetary union (Werner Report) and the other on political union (Davignon Report). This document is an extract from the final communiqué of The Hague summit.

8   They have reaffirmed their readiness to expedite the further action needed to strengthen the Community and promote its development into an economic union. They are of the opinion that the integration process should result in a Community of stability and growth. To this end they agreed that, within the Council, on the basis of the memorandum presented by the Commission on 12 February 1969, and in close collaboration with the latter, a plan in stages will be worked out during 1970 with a view to the creation of an economic and monetary union.

13   They reaffirmed their agreement on the principle of enlargement of the Community, in accordance with Article 237 of the Treaty of Rome.

   In so far as the applicant States accept the Treaties and their political aims, the decisions taken since the entry into force of the Treaties and the options adopted in the sphere of development, the Heads of State or Government have indicated their agreement to the opening of negotiations between the Community on the one hand and the applicant States on the other.

15   They instructed the Ministers for Foreign Affairs to study the best way of achieving progress in the matter of political unification, within the context of enlargement. The Ministers are to make proposals to this effect by the end of July 1970 . . .

Bulletin of the European Economic Community, 1970, No.1,

pp.11–16

DOCUMENT 23   THE WERNER REPORT. CONCLUSIONS FROM THE
REPORT OF THE AD HOC COMMITTEE HEADED
BY PIERRE WERNER ON THE REALISATION BY
STAGES OF ECONOMIC AND MONETARY UNION
IN THE COMMUNITY, LUXEMBOURG,
OCTOBER 1970

*The October 1970 Werner Report outlined a three-stage process for the
creation of a monetary union by 1980: the irrevocable conversion of the
currencies of member states, the free movement of capital, the permanent
locking of exchange rates and the potential of replacing individual national
currencies with a single currency. The report helped to inspire initiatives such
as the 1971 European currency management system (the Snake). However,
the absence of stable currencies meant that the objective of monetary integration became less likely.*

A. Economic and monetary union is an objective realisable in the course
    of the present decade provided only that the political will of the member
    states to realise this objective, as solemnly declared at the Conference at
    The Hague, is present . . .
B. Economic and monetary union means that the principal decisions of
    economic policy will be taken at Community level and therefore that the
    necessary powers will be transferred from the national plane to the Com-
    munity plane. These transfers of responsibility and the creation of the
    corresponding Community institutions represent a process of fundamen-
    tal political significance which entails the progressive development of
    political cooperation . . .
C. A monetary union implies, internally, the total and irreversibly convert-
    ibility of currencies, the elimination of margins of fluctuation in rates of
    exchange, the irrevocable fixing of parity ratios and the total liberation of
    movements of capital . . .
D. On the institutional plane, in the final stage, two Community organs are
    indispensable: a centre of decision for economic policy and a Community
    system for the central banks . . .
E. . . . the development of monetary unification will have to be combined
    with parallel progress towards the harmonisation and finally the unifica-
    tion of economic policies.
F. At this stage the laying down of a precise and concrete timetable for
    the whole of the plane by stages does not seem feasible . . . Particular
    emphasis should therefore be placed on the first stage, for which a pack-
    age of concrete measures is presented. The decisions on the details of the
    final stages and the future timetable will have to be taken at the end of
    the first stage.

G. The first stage will commence on 1 January 1971 and will cover a period of three years . . .

Bulletin of the European Economic Community, 1970, Supplement 11, pp.26–9

DOCUMENT 24   **THE DAVIGNON REPORT. REPORT ON THE PROBLEMS OF POLITICAL UNIFICATION PREPARED BY THE DAVIGNON COMMITTEE AND ADOPTED BY THE FOREIGN MINISTERS OF THE EC MEMBER STATES, LUXEMBOURG, 27 OCTOBER 1970**

The Davignon Report recommended the establishment of a European Political Co-operation (EPC) arrangement to facilitate foreign policy harmonisation and co-ordination among member states. It further proposed that foreign ministers hold two formal meetings every six months (adopted at the 1970 Luxembourg Council meeting) and highlighted a move towards intergovernmentalism within the Community.

PART ONE

1 The Foreign Ministers of the member states of the European Communities were instructed by the Heads of State or Government meeting at The Hague on 1 and 2 December 1969 'to study the best way of achieving progress in the matter of political unification, within the context of enlargement' of the European Communities . . .

6 The Ministers therefore considered that their proposals should be based on three facts, in order to ensure consistency with the continuity and political purpose of the European design which were emphasised so forcefully by the Hague Conference.

7 The first fact is that, in line with the spirit of the Preambles of the Treaties of Paris and Rome, tangible form should be given to the will for a political union, which has always been a force for the progress of the European Communities.

8 The second fact is that the implementation of the common policies being introduced or already in force requires corresponding developments in the specifically political sphere, so as to bring nearer the day when Europeans can speak with one voice. Hence the importance of Europe being built by successive stages and the gradual development of the method and instruments best calculated to allow a common political course of action.

9 The third and final fact is that Europe must prepare itself to discharge the imperative world duties entailed by its greater cohesion and increasing role.

10 Current developments in the European Communities make it necessary for the member states to step up their political cooperation and, in the initial stage, to provide themselves with ways and means of harmonising their views in the field of international politics.

The Ministers therefore felt that foreign-policy concentration should be the object of the first practical endeavours to demonstrate to all that Europe has a political vocation . . .

PART TWO

Being concerned to achieve progress towards political unification, the Governments should decide to cooperate in the field of foreign policy.

I. Objectives
This cooperation has two objectives:

(a) To ensure mutual understanding with respect to the major issues of international politics, by exchanging information and consulting regularly;
(b) To increase their solidarity by working for a harmonisation of views, concentration of attitudes and joint action when it appears feasible and desirable.

Bulletin of the European Economic Community, 1970, No.11, pp.9–12

DOCUMENT 25 **EUROPEAN MONETARY COOPERATION: THE SNAKE. RESOLUTION OF THE COUNCIL OF MINISTERS, BRUSSELS, 21 MARCH 1972**

This document was an agreement by member states to narrow the margin of fluctuation of their currencies against the US dollar by 1.25 per cent on either side, with the tunnel being the limit to which currencies could fluctuate while the Snake referred to the line that currencies created as they increased and decreased. Unstable currencies had a severe impact on the success of the Snake (within two months of the launching of the Snake, sterling was set free to float on 23 June 1972, while Denmark withdrew on 27 June).

1 As a first step towards the establishment of a distinct monetary zone within the framework of the international system, the Council urges the Central Banks of the member states to reduce progressively, while making full use of the fluctuation margins allowed by the IMF on a world plane, the gap existing at any given moment between the exchange rates of the strongest and the weakest currencies of the member states.

To this end, for a period during which these procedures will be tested, the Central Banks are asked to intervene on their respective foreign-exchange markets in accordance with the following principles:

(a) As from a date to be fixed by the Governors of the Central Banks, interventions shall be effected in Community currencies, on the basis of the margins recorded on the market at that date;

(b) As these limits converge the margins mentioned under (a) above shall be narrowed down and shall no longer be widened;

(c) By 1st July 1972 at the latest, the gap existing at any given time between the currencies of two member states may not exceed 2.25 per cent.

2   To this end, the Central Banks are asked to intervene in the foreign currency markets of their own countries, in accordance with the following principles:

*   in community currencies, if their levels reach, on the foreign-currency market involved, the maximum limit of fluctuation authorised under Point 1;

*   in US dollars, if the rate of exchange of the dollar reaches, on the foreign-exchange markets involved, the maximum fluctuation limit authorised under IMF rules;

*   within these fluctuation limits, only after a concerted decision of the Central Banks.

Bulletin of the European Communities, 1972, No.4, pp.43–4

DOCUMENT 26   **ESTABLISHING THE EUROPEAN COUNCIL. COMMUNIQUE OF THE MEETING OF THE HEADS OF STATE OR GOVERNMENT OF THE COMMUNITY, PARIS, 9–10 DECEMBER 1974**

The 1974 Paris summit established a European Council to be comprised of Heads of State or Government of the member states (assisted by their Foreign Minister) and the President of the European Commission. Over time the European Council has acted as political decision-making body and provided impetus to the development of the Community by issuing deadlines and establishing priorities.

1   Recognising the need for an overall approach to the internal problems involved in achieving European unity and the external problems facing Europe, the Heads of Government consider it essential to ensure progress and overall consistency in the activities of the Communities and in the work on political cooperation.

2   The Heads of Government have therefore decided to meet, accompanied by the Ministers of Foreign Affairs, three times a year and whenever

necessary, in the Council of the Communities in the context of political cooperation . . .

3   With a view to progress towards European unity, the Heads of Government reaffirm their determination gradually to adopt a common position and coordinate their diplomatic action in all areas of international affairs which affect the interests of the European Community. The President-in-office will be the spokesman for the Nine and will set out their views in international diplomacy . . .

7   In order to improve the functioning of the Council of the Community, they consider that it is necessary to renounce the practice which consists of making agreement on all questions conditional on the unanimous consent of the member states, whatever their respective position may be regarding the conclusions reached in Luxembourg on 28 January 1966.

8   Greater latitude will be given to the Permanent Representatives so that only the most important political problems will be discussed in the Council.

Eighth General Report EC (1974), p.297

DOCUMENT 27   **THE TINDEMANS REPORT ON EUROPEAN UNION. EXTRACTS FROM BELGIAN PRIME MINISTER LEO TINDEMAN'S LETTER TO HIS EUROPEAN COLLEAGUES, BRUSSELS, 29 DECEMBER 1975**

The Tindemans Report analysed the ways in which a more integrated Europe could be achieved that was also closer to the citizen. This included proposals to reduce the number of Commissioners and a move away from unanimity voting to qualified majority voting. A particularly controversial aspect of the report was its raising of the suggestion of a 'two-speed Europe', whereby there would be different rates of integration within Europe depending on the particular ability and the will of individual member states.

For me, European Union is a new phase in the history of the unification of Europe, which can only be achieved by a continuous process. Consequently, it is difficult to lay down, at this stage, the date of completion of the European Union. It will only achieve its objectives by means of institutions which have been strengthened and improved that the Union will be able to give increasing expression to its own dynamism. In this respect, the role of a directly-elected European Parliament will be decisive in the development of the Union. Finally, I am convinced of the need, in 1980, to assess what we have already achieved so as to open up new prospects and make further progress . . .

Bulletin of the European Communities, 1976, Supplement No.1, pp.14–22

This document sets out the decision of member states to establish a European Monetary System (EMS). The initiative came from German Chancellor Helmut Schmidt and French President Valery Giscard d'Estaing.

1.2   Today, after careful examination of the preparatory work done by the Council and other Community bodies, we are agreed as follows:

A European Monetary System (EMS) will be set up on 1 January 1979.

1.3   We are firmly resolved to ensure the lasting success of the EMS by policies conducive to greater stability at home and abroad for both deficit and surplus countries.

2.1   A European currency unit (ECU) will be at the centre of the EMS. The value and composition of the ECU will be identical with the value of the EUA at the outset of the system.

2.2   The ECU will be used:

(a)   as the denominator (numeraire) for the exchange rate mechanism;

(b)   as the basis for a divergence indicator;

(c)   as the denominator for operations in both the intervention and the credit mechanisms;

(d)   as a means of settlement between monetary authorities of the European Community.

3.1   Each country will have an ECU-related central rate. These central rates will be used to establish a grid of bilateral exchange rates.

Around these exchange rate fluctuation margins of +/–2.25 per cent will be established. EEC countries with presently floating currencies may opt for wider margins up to +/–6 per cent at the outset of the EMS: these margins should be gradually reduced as soon as economic conditions permit.

A Member State which does not participate in the exchange rate mechanism at the outset may participate at a later date . . .

3.4   Intervention in the participating countries is compulsory when the intervention points defined by the fluctuation margins are reached.

http://aei.pitt.edu/archive/0001424/01/Brussels_dec_1978.pdf

DOCUMENT 29 **THE EEC COURT OF JUSTICE AND THE FREE MOVEMENT OF GOODS. THE CASSIS DE DIJON DECISION, LUXEMBOURG, 20 FEBRUARY 1979**

The European Court of Justice ruled that it was not possible for restrictions to be imposed on a product lawfully manufactured and on sale in one member state when it was imported into another member state so long as basic health and safety standards were met.

14 It is clear from the foregoing that the requirements relating to the minimum alcohol content of alcoholic beverages do not serve a purpose which is in the general interest and such as to take precedence over the requirements of the free movement of goods, which constitutes one of the fundamental rules of the Community.

....There is therefore no valid reason why, provided that they have been lawfully produced and marketed in one of the member states, alcoholic beverages should not be introduced into any other Member State; the sale of such products may not be subject to a legal prohibition on the marketing of beverages with an alcohol content lower than the limit set by the national rules.

Report of Cases before the Court, 1979, Part 1, case 120/78, judgment of the
Court of 20 February 1979, pp.660–5

DOCUMENT 30 **BRITISH BUDGET PROBLEM**

These documents reflect on the British budget question which Margaret Thatcher's government sought to resolve (a). Thatcher regularly approached this issue in a combative style (b). A suitable agreement was finally reached at the Fontainebleau European Council of 25–26 June 1984.

(a)

In spite of North Sea oil, by 1979 Britain had become one of the least prosperous members of the Community, with only the seventh highest GDP per head of population among the member states. Yet we were expected shortly to become the largest net contributor.

So from the first my policy was to seek to limit the damage and distortions caused by the CAP and to bring financial realities to bear on Community spending.

Margaret Thatcher (1993) *The Downing Street Years* (London: HarperCollins), p.63

(b)

The Council started at 3.40 . . . There was a certain amount of routine stuff . . . Then into the budget question about 6 o'clock, introduced briefly by me. Mrs. Thatcher did quite well for once, a bit shrill as usual, but not excessively so. There was quite a good initial response . . . Then towards the end Mrs. Thatcher got the question bogged down by being far too demanding. Her mistake, which fed on itself subsequently at dinner and indeed the next morning, arose out of her having only one of the three necessary qualities of a great advocate. She has nerve and determination to win, but she certainly does not have a good understanding of the case against her (which was based on the own-resources theory, of theology if you like), which means that the constantly reiterated cry of 'It's my money I want back' strikes an insistently jarring note . . . She also lacks the third quality, which is that of not boring the judge or jury, and she bored everybody endlessly by only understanding about four of the fourteen or so points on the British side and repeating each of them twenty-seven times.

Roy Jenkins (1989) *European Diary*, 1977–1981 (London: Collins), pp.528–9

DOCUMENT 31   **THE SINGLE EUROPEAN ACT**

These documents concern the act that was agreed at the December 1985 Luxembourg European Council and formally signed in February 1986. It provided for several areas of reform (a). This included the setting of a deadline of 31 December 1992 for the establishment of an internal market. Although Britain welcomed the internal market, the government expressed concerns over plans to increase the powers of the Commission and extend the scope of Community policy-making (b).

(a)

Article 2
The European Council shall bring together the Heads of State or of Government of the member states and the President of the Commission of the European Communities. They shall be assisted by the Ministers for Foreign Affairs and by a Member of the Commission.
    The European Council shall meet at least twice a year.

Article 13
The EEC Treaty shall be supplemented by the following provisions:

'*Article 8A*

The Community shall adopt measures with the aim of progressively estab-lishing the internal market over a period expiring on 31 December 1992, . . .

The internal market shall comprise an area without internal frontiers in which the free movement of goods, persons, services and capital is ensured in accordance with the provisions of this Treaty.'

Article 18
The EEC Treaty shall be supplemented by the following provisions:

'*Article 100A*

1. . . . The Council shall, acting by a qualified majority on a proposal from the Commission in cooperation with the European Parliament and the Economic and Social Committee, adopt measures for the approximation of the provisions laid down by law, regulation or administrative action in member states which have as their object the establishment and function-ing of the internal market . . .'

Single European Act, Luxembourg: Office for Official
Publications of the European Communities, 1986
http://europa.eu.int/abc/obj/treaties/en/entoc113.htm

(b)

The fruits of what would be called the Single European Act were good for Britain. At last, I felt, we were going to get the Community back on course, concentrating on its role as a huge market, with all the opportunities that would bring to our industries . . . The trouble was . . . that the new powers the Commission received only seemed to whet its appetite.

Margaret Thatcher (1993) *The Downing Street Years*
(London: HarperCollins), p.556

DOCUMENT 32   **COMPLETING THE INTERNAL MARKET**

Although the European internal market is the largest market in the world, the scope and degree of implementation of internal market legislation in member states is not wholly complete. In 2002 only 5 of the 15 EU member states (Denmark, Finland, Netherlands, Sweden and the UK) met the European Council's target of a deficit of 1.5 per cent or less.

Member state implementation deficits of internal market laws (percentage) as at 1 October 2002

Country	Percentage deficit
France	3.8%
Greece	3.3%
Portugal	3.1%
Austria	2.9%
Germany	2.7%
Italy	2.6%
Ireland	2.6%
Luxembourg	2.3%
Belgium	2.1%
Spain	1.6%
UK	1.4%
Netherlands	1.3%
Denmark	0.7%
Finland	0.6%
Sweden	0.4%

Internal Market Scoreboard, European Commission

http://www.europa.eu.int/rapid/start/cgi/guesten.ksh?p_action.gettxt=gt&doc=IP/02/
1644|0|RAPID&lg=EN&display=

DOCUMENT 33   **SPEECH GIVEN BY THE BRITISH PRIME MINISTER, MARGARET THATCHER, AT THE COLLEGE OF EUROPE, BRUGES, 20 SEPTEMBER 1988**

This document sets out former Prime Minister Margaret Thatcher's hostility against the European Commission's desire to put in place too many rules and regulations that impacted on member states.

. . . And let me be quite clear. Britain does not dream of some cosy, isolated existence on the fringes of the European Community. Our destiny is in Europe, as part of the Community . . .

. . . My first guiding principle is this: willing and active cooperation between independent sovereign states is the best way to build a successful European Community. To try to suppress nationhood and concentrate power at the centre of a European conglomerate would be highly damaging and would jeopardise the objectives we seek to achieve. Europe will be stronger precisely because it has France as France, Spain as Spain, Britain as Britain, each with its own customs, traditions and identity. It would be folly to try to fit them into some sort of Identikit European personality . . .

. . . working more closely together does *not* require power to be centralised in Brussels or decisions to be taken by an appointed bureaucracy . . . We have not successfully rolled back the frontiers of the state in Britain only to see them re-imposed at a European level, with a European super-state exercising a new dominance from Brussels.

Certainly we want to see Europe more united with a greater sense of common purpose. But it must be in a way which preserves the different traditions, Parliamentary powers and sense of national pride in one's own country; for these have been the source of Europe's vitality through the centuries.

Margaret Thatcher (1997) *The Collected Speeches* (London: HarperCollins), pp.315–25

DOCUMENT 34   **THE DELORS REPORT ON MONETARY UNION**

The Delors Report set out a three-stage transition to monetary union that would culminate in a single currency and a European Central Bank. Phase 1 of the report (1990–93) provided for the consolidation of the single market. Phase 2 (1994–98) included the creation of the European Monetary Institute (EMI), economic convergence and increased monetary cooperation. Phase 3 (1999–2002) included the introduction of a single European currency. In this document, the British Prime Minister Margaret Thatcher sets out her hostility towards the Delors Report.

. . . When the Delors Report finally appeared in April 1989 it confirmed our worst fears. From the beginning there had been discussion of a 'three-stage' approach, which might at least have allowed us to slow the pace and refuse to 'advance' further than the first or second stage. But the report now insisted that by embarking on the first stage the Community committed itself irrevocably to the eventual achievement of full economic and monetary union. There was a requirement for a new treaty and for work on it to start immediately. There was also plenty of material in the treaty about regional and social policy – costly, Delorism socialism on a continental scale. None of these was acceptable to me.

Margaret Thatcher (1993) *The Downing Street Years* (London: HarperCollins), p.708

DOCUMENT 35 **LAUNCHING EUROPEAN POLITICAL UNION.
LETTER WRITTEN BY THE GERMAN CHANCELLOR
HELMUT KOHL AND THE FRENCH PRESIDENT
FRANÇOIS MITTERRAND TO THE IRISH
PRESIDENCY OF THE EC, 19 APRIL 1990**

*The Kohl–Mitterrand letter proved to be a central factor in moving member
states to agree on the need to convene a further IGC on political union. Much
of the pressure for change had come from external events, including the fall of
the Berlin Wall on 11 November 1989, the ensuing collapse of Communism in
Eastern Europe, fragmentation of the Soviet Union and German reunification.*

In the light of far reaching changes in Europe and in view of the completion of
the single market and the realisation of economic and monetary union, we
consider it necessary to accelerate the political construction of the Europe of
the Twelve. We believe that it is time to transform the relations as a whole
among the member states into a European Union . . . and invest this union
with the necessary means of action, as envisaged by the Single Act. With this
in mind, we would like to see the European Council deciding as follows on
28 April:

(1) The European Council should ask the competent bodies to intensify
    the preparations for the intergovernmental conference on economic and
    monetary union, which will be opened by the end of 1990 at the invita-
    tion of the Italian presidency, as decided by the European Council in
    Strasbourg.
(2) The European Council should initiate preparations for an intergovern-
    mental conference on political union. In particular, the objective is to:

    • strengthen the democratic legitimation of the union,
    • render institutions more efficient,
    • ensure unity and coherence of the union's economic, monetary and
      political action,
    • define and implement a common foreign and security policy.

The Foreign Ministers should be instructed to prepare an initial report for the
meeting of the European Council in June and to submit a final report to the
European Council meeting in December. We wish the intergovernmental
conference on political union to be held parallel to the conference on economic and monetary union.

Our aim is that these fundamental reforms – economic and monetary union
as well as political union – should enter into force on 1 January 1993 after
ratification by the national parliaments.

Bulletin of the European Community, Vol.23, No.4, 1990, point 1.12

DOCUMENT 36 CREATING THE SINGLE CURRENCY

So as to ensure that the economies of member states were fit enough to participate in a single currency, a set of convergence criteria were detailed in the Treaty on European Union (a). The Protocol attached to the Treaty stated that member states should have a budget deficit not exceeding 3 per cent of GDP and a public debt not exceeding 60 per cent of GDP (b). To ensure that member states participating in the single currency would maintain a stable level of economic progress (and therefore not jeopardise the single currency), the December 1996 Dublin European Council set out the conditions of a Stability and Growth Pact that required member states to adhere to detailed fiscal and budgetary measures (c).

(a)

Article 104 (ex Article 104c)

1. Member states shall avoid excessive government deficits.
2. The Commission shall monitor the development of the budgetary situation and of the stock of government debt in the member states with a view to identifying gross errors. In particular it shall examine compliance with budgetary discipline on the basis of the following two criteria:

   a. whether the ratio of the planned or actual government deficit to gross domestic product exceeds a reference value, unless:
      - either the ratio has declined substantially and continuously and reached a level that comes close to the reference value;
      - or, alternatively, the excess over the reference value is only exceptional and temporary and the ratio remains close to the reference value;
   b. whether the ratio of government debt to gross domestic product exceeds a reference value, unless the ratio is sufficiently diminishing and approaching the reference value at a satisfactory pace.

The reference values are specified in the Protocol on the excessive deficit procedure annexed to this Treaty . . .

> *The Excessive Deficit Procedure. Extracts from the consolidated*
> *version of the Treaty establishing the European Community*
> http://europa.eu.int/eur-lex/en/treaties/selected/livre223.html

(b)

Article 1
The reference values referred to in Article 104c(2) of this Treaty are:

- 3 per cent for the ratio of the planned or actual government deficit to gross domestic product at market prices;
- 60 per cent for the ratio of government debt to gross domestic product at market prices.

Protocol (No.5) on the Excessive Deficit Procedure

(c)

II. Ensuring budgetary discipline in Stage 3 of EMU (Stability and Growth Pact)

18.   The Treaty imposes on member states in Stage 3 of EMU an obligation to avoid excessive deficits . . .
19.   To that end, the Council proposes to adopt regulations on the strengthening of surveillance and budgetary discipline and on speeding up and clarifying the excessive deficit procedure. These regulations, combined with a European Council Resolution, will constitute a Stability and Growth Pact . . . Euro area member states will be obliged to submit stability programmes and will be subject to agreed sanctions for failure to act effectively on excessive deficits.

Excessive deficit procedure

26.   Adherence to the objective of sound budgetary positions close to balance or in surplus will allow a Member State to deal with normal cyclical fluctuations while keeping its government deficit within the 3 per cent reference value . . . Once it has decided that an excessive deficit persists, and as long as a Member State has failed to comply with a decision under Treaty Article (EC)104c(9), the Council will, in accordance with paragraph 11 of that Article, impose sanctions on a prescribed scale.
27.   An excess of a government deficit over the 3 per cent reference value shall be considered exceptional when resulting from an unusual event outside the control of the relevant Member State and which has a major impact on the financial position of general government, or when resulting from a severe economic downturn.

Stability and Growth Pact, Annex to Presidency Conclusions,
Dublin European Council, 13–14 December 1996
http://ue.eu.int/en/Info/eurocouncil/index.htm

DEVELOPING A COMMON FOREIGN AND SECURITY POLICY

The creation of a European common foreign and security policy was initially set out in the Treaty on European Union (a). It was not until the Franco–British summit in St Malo, 3–4 December 1998, that the 'sea change' in the UK's objection to the EU acquiring an 'autonomous' military capacity ensured that there was proper grounding for the construction of a European defence identity (b). At the December 1999 Helsinki European Council, member states established some of the detail of the European Security and Defence Policy (c). The Constitutional Treaty that was agreed to by member states at the June 2004 European Council enhanced the level of cooperation on foreign and security policy and strengthened EU defence policy (d).

(a)

Article J.1

1. The Union and its member states shall define and implement a common foreign and security policy, governed by the provisions of this Title and covering all areas of foreign and security policy.
2. The objectives of the common foreign and security policy shall be:

   - to safeguard the common values, fundamental interests and independence of the Union;
   - to strengthen the security of the Union and its member states in all ways;
   - to preserve peace and strengthen international security, in accordance with the principles of the United Nations Charter as well as the principles of the Helsinki Final Act and the objectives of the Paris Charter;
   - to promote international cooperation;
   - to develop and consolidate democracy and the rule of law, and respect for human rights and fundamental freedoms . . .

Article J.4

1. The common foreign and security policy shall include all questions related to the security of the Union, including the eventual framing of a common defence policy, which might in time lead to a common defence.
2. The Union requests the Western European Union (WEU), which is an integral part of the development of the Union, to elaborate and implement decisions and actions of the Union which have defence implications. The

Council shall, in agreement with the institutions of the WEU, adopt the necessary practical arrangements.

(b)

1. The European Union needs to be in a position to play its full role on the international stage . . .
2. . . . the Union must have the capacity for autonomous action, backed up by credible military forces, the means to decide to use them, and a readiness to do so, in order to respond to international crises . . .
3. . . . the Union must be given appropriate structures and a capacity for analysis of situations, sources of intelligence, and a capacity for relevant strategic planning . . .
4. Europe needs strengthened armed forces that can react rapidly to the new risks . . .

The Franco–British summit, St Malo, 3–4 December 1998

(c)

Common European Policy on Security and Defence

27. The European Council underlines its determination to develop an autonomous capacity to take decisions and, where NATO as a whole is not engaged, to launch and conduct EU-led military operations in response to international crises. This process will avoid unnecessary duplication and does not imply the creation of a European army.
28. Building on the guidelines established at the Cologne European Council and on the basis of the Presidency's reports, the European Council has agreed in particular the following:

    – cooperating voluntarily in EU-led operations, member states must be able, by 2003, to deploy within 60 days and sustain for at least 1 year military forces of up to 50,000–60,000 persons capable of the full range of Petersberg tasks;
    – new political and military bodies and structures will be established within the Council to enable the Union to ensure the necessary political guidance and strategic direction to such operations, while respecting the single institutional framework;
    – modalities will be developed for full consultation, cooperation and transparency between the EU and NATO, taking into account the needs of all EU member states;
    – appropriate arrangements will be defined that would allow, while respecting the Union's decision-making autonomy, non-EU European NATO members and other interested States to contribute to EU military crisis management;

- a non-military crisis management mechanism will be established to coordinate and make more effective the various civilian means and resources, in parallel with the military ones, at the disposal of the Union and the member states.

Extracts from the conclusions of the European Council in Helsinki,
10–11 December 1999. http://Ue.Eu.Int/En/Info/Eurocouncil/Index.Htm

(d)

Specific provisions relating to the common security and defence policy

Article I-41

1. The common security and defence policy shall be an integral part of the common foreign and security policy. It shall provide the Union with an operational capacity drawing on civil and military assets. The Union may use them on mission outside the Union for peace-keeping, conflict prevention and strengthening the international security in accordance with the principles of the United Nations Charter. The performance of these tasks shall be undertaken using capabilities provided by the member states.

2. The common security and defence policy shall include the progressive framing of a common Union defence policy. This will lead to a common defence, when the European Council, acting unanimously, so decides. It shall in that case recommend to the member states the adoption of such a decision in accordance with their respective constitutional requirements.

The policy of the Union in accordance with this Article shall not prejudice the specific character of the security and defence policy of certain member states, it shall respect the obligations of certain member states, which see their common defence realised in the North Atlantic Treaty Organisation, under the North Atlantic Treaty, and be compatible with the common security and defence policy established within that framework.

3. Member states shall make civilian and military capabilities available to the Union for the implementation of the common security and defence policy, to contribute to the objectives defined by the Council. Those member states which together establish multinational forces may also make them available to the common security and defence policy.

Member states shall undertake progressively to improve their military capabilities. An Agency in the field of defence capabilities, research, acquisition and armaments (European Defence Agency) shall be established to identify operational requirements, to promote measures to satisfy those requirements, to contribute to identifying and, where appropriate, implementing any measure needed to strengthen the industrial and technological base of the defence sector, to participate in defining a European capabilities and armaments policy, and to assist the Council in evaluating the improvement of military capabilities.

4. European decisions relating to the common security and defence policy, including those initiating a mission as referred to in this Article, shall be adopted by the Council acting unanimously on a proposal from the Union Minister for Foreign Affairs or an initiative from a member state. The Union Minister for Foreign Affairs may propose the use of both national resources and Union instruments, together with the Commission where appropriate.
5. The Council may entrust the execution of a task, within the Union framework, to a group of member states in order to protect the Union's values and serve its interests . . .
6. Those member states whose military capabilities fulfil higher criteria and which have made more binding commitments to one another in this area with a view to the most demanding missions shall establish permanent structured cooperation within the Union framework . . .

> *Treaty Establishing a Constitution for Europe*, 6 August 2004
> http://ue.eu.int/igcpdf/en/04/cg00/cg00087.en04.pdf

DOCUMENT 38   **ENLARGING THE EUROPEAN UNION**

In 2004 the membership of the EU enlarged from 15 to 25 member states, its population increased by over 100 million people and its geographical area expanded by 34 per cent. Countries wishing to join the EU have to meet certain criteria that were set out in the Copenhagen European Council of June 1993 (a). At the December 1997 Luxembourg European Council, member states further clarified what the process of enlargement would entail (b). On 9 December 2002 the Commission recommended that negotiations be concluded with Cyprus, the Czech Republic, Estonia, Hungary, Latvia, Lithuania, Malta, Poland, the Slovak Republic and Slovenia (c).

(a)

Membership requires that the candidate country has achieved stability of institutions guaranteeing democracy, the rule of law, human rights and respect for and protection of minorities, the existence of a functioning market economy as well as the capacity to cope with competitive pressure and market forces within the Union. Membership presupposes the candidate's ability to take on the obligations of membership, including adherence to the aims of political, economic and monetary union.

> *Presidency Conclusions, Copenhagen European Council, 21–22 June 1993*

(b)

10. The European Council has considered the current situation in each of the eleven applicant States on the basis of the Commission's opinions and the Presidency's report to the Council. In the light of its discussions, it has decided to launch an accession process comprising the ten Central and East European applicant States and Cyprus. This accession process will form part of the implementation of Article 0 of the Treaty on European Union. The European Council points out that all these States are destined to join the European Union on the basis of the same criteria and that they are participating in the accession process on an equal footing . . .

Presidency Conclusions, Luxembourg European Council, December 1997.
http://ue.eu.int/en/Info/eurocouncil/index.htm

(c)

Overall assessment
The Union endorses the findings and recommendations of the Commission that Cyprus, the Czech Republic, Estonia, Hungary, Latvia, Lithuania, Malta, Poland, the Slovak Republic and Slovenia fulfil the political criteria and will be able to fulfil the economic criteria and to assume the obligations of membership from the beginning of 2004.

Brussels European Council, 24–25 October 2002
http://www.europa.eu.int/rapid/start/cgi/guesten.ksh?p_action.gettxt=gt&doc=
DOC/02/14|0|RAPID&lg=EN;

DOCUMENT 39   **COUNCIL VOTING AND EUROPEAN PARLIAMENT REPRESENTATION POST-NICE**

The enlargement of the European Union prompted a reassessment of the weighting of votes in the Council and the distribution of seats in the European Parliament (a). The Treaty of Nice that was negotiated at the December 2000 Nice European Council listed 29 new policy areas covered by QMV. Some member states were unhappy with the distribution of votes that was the outcome of the Nice Treaty because medium-sized countries like Poland and Spain had greater influence relative to their population than larger countries such as Germany. This prompted member states to reassess the definition of majority voting in the Constitutional Treaty that was agreed in June 2004 (b).

(a)

Country	Population (millions)	Votes in the Council of Ministers		Members of the European Parliament	
		Pre-Nice	Post-Nice	5th term: 1999–2004	6th term: 2004–09
Germany	82.0	10	29	99	99
France	61.0	10	29	87	78
Britain	60.0	10	29	87	78
Italy	58.0	10	29	87	78
Spain	40.2	8	27	64	54
Poland	38.5	0	27	0	54
Netherlands	16.2	5	13	31	27
Greece	10.7	5	12	25	24
Czech Republic	10.3	0	12	0	24
Belgium	10.2	5	12	25	24
Hungary	10.1	0	12	0	24
Portugal	10.0	5	12	25	24
Sweden	8.9	4	10	22	19
Austria	8.1	4	10	21	18
Slovak Republic	5.4	0	7	0	14
Denmark	5.3	3	7	16	14
Finland	5.2	3	7	16	14
Ireland	3.9	3	7	15	13
Lithuania	3.7	0	7	0	13
Latvia	2.4	0	4	0	9
Slovenia	2.0	0	4	0	7
Estonia	1.4	0	4	0	6
Cyprus	0.8	0	4	0	6
Luxembourg	0.4	2	4	6	6
Malta	0.4	0	3	0	5
Totals	455.1	87	321	626	732
	(25 countries)	(15 countries)	(25 countries)	(15 countries)	(25 countries)

(b)

Article I-25
Definition of qualified majority voting within the European Council and Council

1. A qualified majority shall be defined as at least 55 per cent of the members of the Council, comprising at least fifteen of them and representing Member States comprising at least 65 per cent of the population of the Union.

A blocking minority must include at least four Council members, failing which the qualified majority shall be deemed attained.

2. By way of derogation from paragraph 1, when the Council is not acting on a proposal from the Commission or from the Union Minister for

Foreign Affairs, the qualified majority shall be defined as at least 72 per cent of the members of the Council, representing Member States comprising at least 65 per cent of the population.

3. Paragraphs 1 and 2 shall apply to the European Council when it is acting by a qualified majority.

4. Within the Council, its President and the President of the Commission shall not take part in the vote.

Treaty Establishing a Constitution for Europe, 6 August 2004
http://ue.eu.int/igcpdf/en/04/cg00/cg00087.en04.pdf

DOCUMENT 40   **VOTER TURNOUT IN EUROPEAN PARLIAMENT ELECTIONS**

This document chronicles the turnout in European Parliament elections since direct elections were first held in 1979. At the 2004 elections the average level of voting fell for the sixth time running.

State	1979	1981	1984	1987	1989	1994	1995	1996	1999	2004
Belgium	91.4		92.2		90.7	90.7			91	90.81
France	60.7		56.7		48.7	52.7			46.8	42.76
Germany	65.7		56.8		62.3	60.0			45.2	43
Italy	84.9		83.4		81.5	74.8			70.8	73.1
Luxembourg	88.9		88.8		87.4	88.5			87.3	89
Netherlands	57.8		50.6		47.2	35.6			30	39.3
Denmark	47.8		52.4		46.2	52.9			50.5	47.9
Ireland	63.6		47.6		68.3	44.0			50.2	58.8
UK	32.2		32.6		36.2	36.4			24.0	38.83
Greece		78.6	77.2		79.9	71.2			75.3	63.22
Portugal				72.4	51.2	35.5			40	38.6
Spain				68.9	54.6	59.1			63	45.1
Austria								67.7	49.9	42.43
Finland								60.3	31.4	39.4
Sweden							41.6		38.8	37.8
Cyprus										71.19
Czech Republic										28.32
Estonia										26.38
Hungary										38.5
Latvia										41.34
Lithuania										48.38
Malta										82.37
Poland										20.87
Slovakia										16.96
Slovenia										28.3
EU	63		61		58.5	56.8			49.8	45.7

http://www.elections2004.eu.int

DOCUMENT 41   **EU–US RELATIONS**

The United States has a particularly close relationship with the European Union. The context of the relationship was set out in the 1990 Transatlantic Declaration (a). It established a regular series of meetings between heads of state and government and foreign ministers, while the US Under-Secretaries of State for Business and Political Affairs met with their counterparts in the European Commission (external relations). Some years later the 1995 New Transatlantic Agenda set out a list of objectives that were of importance to the EU and the US in terms of bilateral relations as well as in the broader global context (b).

(a)

(...)

To achieve their common goals, the European Community and its member states and the United States of America will inform and consult each other on important matters of common interest, both political and economic, with a view to bringing their positions as close as possible, without prejudice to their respective independence. In appropriate international bodies, in particular, they will seek close cooperation . . .

Transatlantic Declaration, 22 November 1990

(b)

(...)

Today we adopt a New Transatlantic Agenda based on a Framework for Action with four major goals:

1. Promoting peace and stability, democracy and development around the world. Together, we will work for an increasingly stable and prosperous Europe; foster democracy and economic reform in Central and Eastern Europe as well as in Russia, Ukraine and other new independent states; secure peace in the Middle East; advance human rights; promote non-proliferation and cooperate on development and humanitarian assistance.
2. Responding to global challenges. Together, we will fight international crime, drug-trafficking and terrorism; address the needs of refugees and displaced persons; protect the environment and combat disease.
3. Contributing to the expansion of world trade and closer economic relations. Together, we will strengthen the multilateral trading system and take concrete, practical steps to promote closer economic relations between us.
4. Building bridges across the Atlantic. Together, we will work with our business people, scientists, educators and others to improve communication

and to ensure that future generations remain as committed as we are to developing a full and equal partnership.

New Transatlantic Agenda, 1995

DOCUMENT 42 **ENHANCING THE CONSISTENCY OF THE EU'S EXTERNAL ACTION**

Concern that the EU's external competence was hindered by the rotation of the Presidency of the Council on a six-monthly basis among the member states and the overlapping roles of the European Commissioner for External Relations and the EU High Representative for Foreign Policy resulted in changes being introduced in the EU Constitutional Treaty that was agreed to by member states at the Brussels European Council of June 2004. This resulted in agreement on a new post of European Council President (a) and an EU Minister for Foreign Affairs (b).

(a)

Article I-22
The European Council President

1. The European Council shall elect its President, by a qualified majority, for a term of two and a half years, renewable once. In the event of an impediment or serious misconduct, the European Council can end his or her term of office in accordance with the same procedure.
2. The President of the European Council:

    (a) shall chair it and drive forward its work;
    (b) shall ensure the preparation and continuity of the work of the European Council in cooperation with the President of the Commission, and on the basis of the work of the General Affairs Council;
    (c) shall endeavour to facilitate cohesion and consensus within the European Council;
    (d) shall present a report to the European Parliament after each of the meetings of the European Council.

The President of the European Council shall, at his or her level and in that capacity, ensure the external representation of the Union on issues concerning its common foreign and security policy, without prejudice to the powers of the Union Minister for Foreign Affairs.

3. The President of the Council shall not hold a national office.

Treaty Establishing a Constitution for Europe, 6 August 2004
http://ue.eu.int/igcpdf/en/04/cg00/cg00087.en04.pdf

(a)

Article I-28
The Union Minister for Foreign Affairs

1. The European Council, acting by a qualified majority, with the agreement of the President of the Commission, shall appoint the Union Minister for Foreign Affairs. The European Council may end his or her term by the same procedure.
2. The Union Minister for Foreign Affairs shall conduct the Union's common foreign and security policy. He or she shall contribute by his or her proposals to the development of that policy, which he or she shall carry out as mandated by the Council. The same shall apply to the common security and defence policy.
3. The Union Minister for Foreign Affairs shall preside over the Foreign Affairs Council.
4. The Union Minister for Foreign Affairs shall be one of the Vice-Presidents of the Commission. He or she shall ensure the consistency of the Union's external action. He or she shall be responsible for coordinating other aspects of the Union's external action. In exercising these responsibilities within the Commission, and only for these responsibilities, the Union Minister for Foreign Affairs shall be bound by Commission procedures to the extent that this is consistent with paragraphs 2 and 3.

Treaty Establishing a Constitution for Europe, 6 August 2004
http://ue.eu.int/igcpdf/en/04/cg00/cg00087.en04.pdf

GLOSSARY

Accession   The process of joining the EU.

Acquis communautaire   The assortment of legislation, treaties and rulings of the European Court of Justice that constitute the legal identity of the EU. Usually referred to as simply the 'acquis'.

Agenda 2000   Constituted measures to reform the CAP and cohesion policy in response to EU enlargement to Central and Eastern Europe.

Area of Freedom, Security and Justice (AFSJ)   The Treaty of Amsterdam brought the Schengen agreements into the European Community. This provided for the abolition of frontier controls, the free movement of people and cooperation between judicial and police authorities to combat cross-border crime.

Assent procedure   Refers to the procedure whereby the European Parliament's assent, by means of an absolute majority of its members, is necessary before certain important decisions can be adopted.

Association agreement   An agreement between the EU and non-member countries that fosters a close economic and political relationship.

Atlanticism   Refers to a view that the interests of a nation state are maximised by a close relationship with the US.

Barriers to trade   Refer to the elimination of tariffs and quotas among member states.

Brussels Treaty   Signed on 17 March 1948 by Belgium, France, Luxembourg, the Netherlands and the UK to provide a system of collective self-defence.

Co-decision procedure   Introduced in the 1993 Treaty on European Union to increase the powers of the European Parliament whereby it is able to prevent a proposal being adopted if its views are not taken into consideration by the Council.

Cohesion Fund   Introduced in the Treaty on European Union to provide financial assistance to poorer member states.

Cold war   Refers to the rivalry between the US and the Soviet Union after the end of the Second World War, which continued until the collapse of Communism in 1989 and the break-up of the Soviet Union in 1991.

Committee of the Regions   Comprises representatives of local and regional authorities who are appointed by national governments and not directly by any regional authority.

Common Agricultural Policy (CAP)   Established in 1962 to support agricultural production, accounting for approximately 45 per cent of the EU budget.

Common Foreign and Security Policy (CFSP)   Established by the Treaty on European Union to develop the defence and security capacity of the EU.

Consultation procedure   Requires an opinion from the European Parliament before the Council can take a decision.

Convention on the Future of Europe   Established in 2002, chaired by former French President Valéry Giscard d'Estaing. A draft Constitutional Treaty was published in June 2003 which set out possible routes for future European integration in light of the 2004 enlargement of the EU.

Convergence criteria   Refer to the economic conditions that member states have to meet before they can take part in stage three of EMU. The criteria are: (1) an average rate of inflation of not more than 1.5 per cent higher than that of the three best performers; (2) a budget deficit of not more than 3 per cent of GDP and a public debt ratio not exceeding 60 per cent of GDP; (3) in the narrow bands of the ERM for two years without severe tension or devaluation; (4) average nominal long-term interest rate not more than 2 per cent higher than that of the three best-performing states.

Cooperation procedure   Introduced in the SEA to provide the European Parliament with a greater input to the legislative process.

Core Europe   Refers to a small group of countries that are willing to enter into closer cooperation with each other.

Council of Europe   Established in May 1949 to assist with the maintenance of the rules of law and democracy. While it has contributed to fostering European integration, it is not part of the EU. Membership has expanded from 10 to 45 nations.

Council of Ministers   Comprises ministers from member states. It is the main decision-making body of the EU, has legislating and decision-making powers, and should not be confused with the Council of Europe.

Customs Union   When two or more countries establish a free trade policy among themselves by lifting duties and creating a common external tariff.

Decisions   One of three types of binding legislation that is used in the EU (others are directives and regulations). Decisions, which can be adopted by the Council on its own, by the Commission (in certain circumstances) and the Council and the European Parliament (co-decision procedure), are fully binding on those that the decision is applicable to. This could include member states, companies and individuals.

Deepening   Refers to the advances made in European integration from the initial customs union to the creation of the euro zone.

Democratic deficit   The belief that the EU lacks sufficient democratic and parliamentary supervision. It is often used in connection with the desire to increase the powers of the European Parliament.

Directives   One of three types of binding legislation that is used in the EU (others are decisions and regulations). Directives can be adopted by the Council on its own, by the Commission (in certain circumstances) and the Council and the European Parliament (co-decision procedure). They are targeted at member states, requiring them to adopt appropriate legislation, though member states are able to decide on the method and form of implementation.

Economic and Monetary Union (EMU)   A central feature of the TEU. By 1999 11 member states had met the necessary convergence criteria to proceed to a single currency (Greece subsequently joined in 2001).

Empty chair crisis   Refers to a period when the Community was brought to a standstill by France's refusal to participate in meetings of the Council of Ministers between July and December 1965.

Enhanced cooperation   Permits those member states which wish to develop deeper forms of integration than others to do so.

Euro zone   Consists of the member states which have adopted the euro as the single currency.

European Atomic Energy Community (Euratom)   Established in 1957 to develop nuclear energy and conduct research.

European Central Bank (ECB)   Based in Frankfurt and is responsible for the monetary policy of the euro zone. Its main objective is the maintenance of price stability.

European Coal and Steel Community (ECSC)   Provided the first example of supranational cooperation when it commenced operations in 1952.

European Commission   The executive body of the EU and guardian of the Treaties. It has the task of initiating EU legislation, implementing policies that have been agreed on and also plays an important role in negotiating on behalf of the EU on trade matters and with respect to relations with third world countries. It can also refer matters to the ECJ when agreed policies have not been implemented by member states.

European Communities   A phrase that symbolises the ECSC, EEC and Euratom. Since the Merger Treaty of 1967, each of the three Communities have shared the same institutional structure. The 1993 Maastricht Treaty on European Union officially renamed the EEC the European Community (EC), at which time the EC became a central component of the European Union (EU).

European Community   The first pillar of the EU. There are, in fact, three European Communities that have their roots in the individual Treaties that were agreed to in the 1950s. This includes the European Community (being formerly the European Economic Community), the ECSC and the European Atomic Energy Community. The 1967 Merger Treaty brought them into a single institutional structure.

European Council   Comprises heads of state or government of the member states and the president of the European Commission, and provides political direction to the EU.

European Court of Auditors   Monitors the management of the finances of the Community.

European Court of Human Rights   Based in Strasbourg within the Council of Europe and hears cases relating to states that have ratified the European Convention on Human Rights.

European Court of Justice   The final arbiter of all legal issues, including the resolution of disputes between EU member states as well as between firms and individuals within the EU.

European Defence Community (EDC)   An unsuccessful attempt to create a common European army that failed because of the refusal of the French National Assembly to support it in 1954.

European Economic Area (EEA)　Refers to the 1992 agreement that extended the single market to the member countries of the European Free Trade Association (EFTA).

European Economic Community (EEC)　Created by the 1957 Treaty of Rome. It has been revised via the SEA and TEU. When the latter entered into force on 1 January 1993, the EEC was renamed the European Community and formed part of the European Union (EU).

European Free Trade Association (EFTA)　Created in 1960 to provide a less supranational trading group than the EEC. Its relevance has declined as many EFTA members have joined the EU and at the time of writing its membership is limited to Iceland, Liechtenstein, Norway and Switzerland.

European Monetary System (EMS)　Established in 1979 as a 'zone of monetary stability'. It comprised the ERM, which was a parity grid for restricting the fluctuation of currencies, the ECU and the European Monetary Cooperation Fund (EMCF).

European Parliament　Comprises members of the European Parliament (MEPs) who are directly elected for a five-year term of office from each member state, with the number of national MEPs being in proportion to population. The most important area of the European Parliament's influence is its power to amend and adopt legislation via the co-decision procedure, while its approval is also necessary for appointments to the European Commission.

European Political Cooperation (EPC)　Refers to cooperation by EC foreign ministers in the field of foreign policy which began in 1970 and was replaced with the CFSP.

European Union (EU)　Comprises three pillars, the first of which is the EC. The second pillar covers CFSP, while the third pillar (after amendment in the Treaty of Amsterdam) covers cooperation of police and justice authorities in matters of a criminal nature.

Europeanisation　Term that is used to refer to the impact that the EU has had on member states, whereby the pressure of common policies and structures forces a degree of uniformity.

Exchange Rate Mechanism (ERM)　A parity grid where currencies were given a central value in relation to the ECU.

Federalism　In the EU context is a theory of integration that places emphasis on the building of supranational institutions which in turn limit the influence of nation states. Key federalists, such as Jean Monnet, concluded that the conflict of the Second World War had highlighted the need to move beyond the centrality of the nation state in international politics. Thus, the early Treaties of European integration put emphasis on supranational institutions such as the European Commission and European Court of Justice. Some member states, including Britain and France, have often attempted to limit this supranational influence.

Flexibility　A concept that is used to highlight a situation whereby all member states are not committed to a specific EU policy, such as the single currency.

Functionalism　A theory of integration that advocates cooperation between nation states through the creation of organisations that encourage integration in economic, social and technical policies. A theory that is associated with the work of David Mitrany, the functionalist approach does not share the institutional blueprint that is linked with federalism. Functionalists argue that the process of nation states working together in limited policy areas creates benefits that in turn encourage integration to spread by a process of 'spillover' into other policy areas. This functionalist approach was reflected in the plans for the European Coal and Steel Community.

Hard core A view of European integration which includes a small number of member states that seek to cooperate.

Harmonisation The process of bringing states closer together by the setting of common European standards from which they cannot deviate.

High Authority The administrating body of the ECSC and the forerunner of the European Commission.

Intergovernmental conference (IGC) A negotiating forum that comprises representatives of all member states with the aim of making changes to the EU's activities.

Intergovernmentalism An approach to European integration which emphasises the centrality of member states and which seeks to limit the influence of supranational institutions. It therefore contrasts with federalist approaches that aim to enhance the influence of supranational institutions.

Justice and Home Affairs (JHA) Introduced in the TEU to increase cooperation among member states on matters of asylum policy, the crossing of the external borders of member states, immigration policy, combating drugs, combating international fraud, judicial cooperation in civil and criminal matters, customs cooperation and police cooperation.

Liberal intergovernmentalism A theoretical account that places emphasis on the manner in which the EU has been transformed by a series of intergovernmental bargains. This theory states that integration will take place only when there exists enough domestic political support for further integration and when there is a convergence in the preferences of governments.

Marshall Plan Refers to the plan advanced in June 1947 by the US Secretary of State, General George C. Marshall, to improve the economic recovery of European states by means of US financial assistance.

Merger Treaty Established a single Council of Ministers and a single Commission for Euratom, the ECSC and the EEC, which came into force on 1 July 1967.

Multi-level governance Highlights the range of different actors that have an input to EU politics at the European, national and sub-national (regional/local) level.

Multispeed Europe Refers to a situation whereby there are variations in the pace of European integration between member states.

Mutual recognition The principle that a product sold in one EU member state should be able to be sold in any EU member state.

Negative integration A method of European integration that involves the removal of barriers between member states.

Neo-functionalism A theory of European integration that considers the path of integration to be an incremental one that involves the spillover of integration from one sector to another.

Neo-realism A further development on the realist account of international relations which conceptualises the state as a cohesive actor pursuing a set of policies that reflect the national interest.

Net contributors   EU member states that obtain less funding out of the EU than they contribute to its budget.

Net recipients   EU member states that obtain more funding out of the EU than they contribute to its budget.

North Atlantic Treaty Organisation (NATO)   Founded in 1949 and at the time of writing has 19 members. It includes all the EU states (apart from Austria, Finland, Ireland and Sweden), Canada, Iceland, Norway, Turkey and the United States. Since March 1999 it has also included the Czech Republic, Hungary and Poland. At the heart of NATO is an Article 5 Treaty commitment that an attack on one member is an attack on all members and thus in the wake of the September 2001 terrorist attacks on the United States, NATO responded by invoking Article 5. As an organisation NATO has been quicker to respond to the changing geopolitical landscape of Europe than the EU and has expanded its membership to include former Warsaw Pact countries.

Opt-out   Refers to the situation whereby it has been decided that a member state has not wanted to join others in a specific EU policy area.

Organisation for European Economic Cooperation (OEEC)   Established in 1948 to administer assistance provided by the Marshall Plan to Western European countries.

Own resources   Refers to the 1970 decision to provide the Community with a degree of financial autonomy from member states, whereby the Community would obtain revenues directly from agricultural duties, customs duties and a VAT resource.

Pillars   Refer to the three pillars of the EU. The EC is pillar one, which includes the EEC, the ECSC and Euratom. The second pillar is the CFSP and the third pillar is JHA. Pillars two and three permit intergovernmental cooperation and do not include the supranational cooperation of the first pillar.

Positive integration   Refers to a form of integration that involves the creation of policies and institutions.

Price support mechanism   The system of agricultural support for farmers that results in higher food prices.

Qualified majority voting (QMV)   A process of decision-taking where it is possible for decisions to be passed if there is sufficient backing for the initiative, with votes being divided among member states in proportion to their relative size.

Realism   A theory which considers power to be the key factor that shapes human action and which considers that states are the primary actors in international relations.

Regulations   One of three binding forms of EU legislation (others are decisions and directives). Regulations, which can by adopted by the Council on its own, by the Commission (in certain circumstances) and the Council and the European Parliament (co-decision procedure), are directly applicable and fully binding on those that the regulation is applicable to. This includes the administrations of member states.

Resolutions   A method that the Council uses to highlight a political commitment and does not require any need for binding legislation. They do not require the Commission to propose them.

Schengen Agreement   Signed in the Luxembourg town of Schengen in 1985 so as to remove border controls between EU member states. The initial signature countries were Belgium, France, Germany, Luxembourg, the Netherlands, Portugal and Spain. The Agreement (which was initially outside the EC) was incorporated into it by the Treaty of Amsterdam.

Schuman Plan   Signed on 9 May 1950 and resulted in the establishment of the European Coal and Steel Community.

Sectoral integration   A view of integration that takes an incremental approach sector by sector.

Single European Act (SEA)   Played a key role in advancing the single market programme, widening the scope of the competence of the EC and advancing the cause of Economic and Monetary Union.

Single European Market (SEM)   Refers to 'an area without frontiers in which the free movement of goods, persons, services and capital is ensured'.

Snake in the tunnel   A March 1972 agreement that limited the fluctuation of currencies of European nations by means of restricting movement against the US dollar at a rate of 1.25 per cent on either side.

Spillover   Refers to the neo-functionalist view that sectoral integration on one area would have an impact on other areas.

Stability and Growth Pact   A set of regulations to ensure the application of the TEU's provision on the excessive deficit procedure. The pact requires member states to adhere to a strict set of economic policies so as to ensure that they are able to meet the necessary requirements for progression towards the single currency.

State aids   Refers to the situation where EU competition policy prohibits member state governments from subsidising companies through state aids as this clearly provides them with an unfair advantage.

Structural funds   Promote cohesion between EU member states. Structural funds are the European Social Fund, the European Regional and Development Fund and the guidance section of the European Agricultural Guidance and Guarantee Fund.

Subsidiarity   The concept that action should be taken at the level of the Community only if it is not possible to deal with the policy at a national level.

Supranationalism   Whereby national governments share sovereignty with institutions that span all parties, of which the laws of the institutions are binding on the national governments.

Third countries   Refer to any state that is not a member of the EU.

Transparency   Refers to the degree of openness within the EU institutions.

Transposition   The process whereby Community law is written into national legislation, being required for Directives.

Treaty of Amsterdam, 1997   Widened the scope of the co-decision procedure, increased the use of qualified majority voting, improved the effectiveness of foreign policy cooperation, incorporated the Schengen Agreement into the Community and established an employment chapter.

Treaty of Nice, 2000   Focused on the weighting of votes in the Council for decisions by a qualified majority, deciding that the system of QMV decision-taking would be changed from 1 January 2005.

Treaty of Paris, 1951   By Belgium, France, West Germany, Italy, Luxembourg and the Netherlands (the 'Six') and which established the European Coal and Steel Community (ECSC) that came into operation in 1952.

Treaty of Rome, 1957   Established the European Economic Community (EEC) and the European Atomic Energy Community (Euratom).

Treaty on European Union (TEU), 1993   (The Maastricht Treaty) Increased the powers of the European Parliament and set a deadline for EMU.

Truman Doctrine   Refers to the commitment made by US President Truman in March 1947 to maintain freedom throughout the world by limiting the spread of Communism.

Unanimity   One of three forms of voting in the Council. Requires that no member state can vote against a proposal, though it is possible to have abstentions.

Variable geometry   Refers to a concept of integration that permits some member states to make further advances while others remain isolated from these areas of policy-making.

Werner Report, 1970   Set out a three-stage process for the creation of EMU within a period of ten years.

WHO'S WHO

Acheson, Dean (1893–1971) Served as US Secretary of State from 1949 to 1953 during which time he was a strong supporter of NATO and the policy of containment.

Adenauer, Konrad (1876–1967) First Chancellor of the Federal Republic of Germany from 1949 to his resignation in 1963. Negotiated German entry into the EEC and NATO and developed a close relationship with France, resulting in the 1963 Treaty of Friendship between the two nations.

Barroso, José Manuel (1956–) President of the European Commission since 1 November 2004. Previously Prime Minister and Foreign Minister of Portugal.

Bevin, Ernest (1897–1976) UK Labour Foreign Secretary from 1945 until his resignation on ill-health grounds in 1951. Played an influential role in the Brussels Treaty and Britain's entry to NATO.

Bidault, Georges (1899–1983) Served as French Foreign Minister under de Gaulle. Although he played an important role in the creation of the OEEC and NATO, he was primarily concerned with Germany's revival.

Blair, Anthony (1953–) UK Prime Minister since 1997. A committed pro-European, he has attempted to raise the UK's profile in Europe and has been particularly active in developing a stronger European security and defence policy.

Brandt, Willy (1913–92) Socialist Chancellor of the Federal Republic of Germany from 1969 until his resignation in 1974. Was leader of the Social Democratic Party (SDP) from 1964 to 1987. Developed an active foreign policy towards Eastern Europe and the Soviet Union (referred to as *Ostpolitik*).

Briand, Aristide (1862–1932) A key Socialist politician who served as Prime Minister and Foreign Minister in the French Third Republic. As French Foreign Minister, he was one of the first advocates of a European Federal Union and proposed such a scheme to the League of Nations on 5 September 1929. But while the French government circulated a memorandum in May 1930 that set out Briand's proposals in more detail, a combination of a lack of support from other member states and Briand's death in 1932 brought to an end the proposals.

Chirac, Jacques (1932–) Gaullist politician and President of France since 1995 having previously been Prime Minister from 1974 to 1976 and 1986 to 1988.

Churchill, Sir Winston (1874–1965) Served as Prime Minister from 1940 to 1945 and 1951 to 1955 (8 years and 240 days in total). After the landslide Labour Party victory in the 1945 general election, he led the Conservative Party in opposition, during which time he advocated closer European integration, urging for the construction of a United States of Europe in 1946.

Cockfield, Francis (Baron) (1916–) UK Conservative Secretary of State for Trade from 1982 to 1983. Member of the European Commission with responsibility for the Internal Market from 1985 to 1988.

Davignon, Viscount Etienne (1932–) As political director of the Belgian foreign ministry in the 1970s he chaired the committee which devised the report that laid the foundations of European Political Cooperation (EPC). Promoted greater competitiveness among member states during his period as a member of the European Commission from 1977 to 1985.

De Gasperi, Alcide (1881–1954) One of the founding fathers of Europe, he led eight Italian governments between 1945 and 1953. Played a key role in cementing Italy's position in Europe after the war, which resulted in Italy joining NATO and the ECSC.

De Gaulle, Charles (1890–1970) Leader of the Free French during the Second World War and President of France from 1958 to 1969. Attached great emphasis to European integration, partly as a means of lessening the reliance on the US, although his attachment to the importance of national sovereignty threw the Community into crisis with the French boycott in the Council of Ministers from January until June 1965. De Gaulle is also famous for having vetoed UK applications to join the Community in 1963 and 1967.

Delors, Jacques (1925–) President of the European Commission from 1985 to 1995. Played a significant role in developing the EEC, both in terms of widening membership and increasing the scope of the policies it embraced.

Duisenberg, Willem (1935–) First President of the European Central Bank (ECB) from June 1998 to October 2003, having previously been a Council member of the European Monetary Institute (the forerunner of the ECB) from 1994 to 1997.

Eden, Anthony (1897–1977) UK Prime Minister from 1955 to 1957, during which time he played a key role in the rearmament of Germany and its entry into NATO in 1955. His resignation in 1957 was influenced by his actions in the 1956 Suez crisis.

Erhard, Ludwig (1897–1977) Played a central role in Germany's economic recovery after 1949, and served as Chancellor from 1963–1966.

Genscher, Hans-Dietrich (1927–) Foreign Minister of the Federal Republic of Germany from 1974 to 1992. Was the main architect of the 1981 Genscher-Colombo Plan.

Giscard d'Estaing, Valéry (1926–) President of France from 1974 to 1981. Influential in the institutionalisation of summit meetings of Community heads of state and government and supported the development of the European Monetary System. Chaired the discussions on the Convention on the future of Europe that took place between March 2002 and June 2003.

Gorbachev, Mikhail (1931–) General Secretary of the Soviet Union from 1985 until his resignation in 1991. He was instrumental in the change in Soviet policy that was reflected in the policies of *glasnost* and *perestroika*. Established close relations with the United States and Western Europe.

Hallstein, Walter (1901–82) First President of the European Commission, holding office from 1958 to 1967. His views often clashed with those of the French President, Charles de Gaulle, who did not share Hallstein's desire for the Commission to be the main motor of European integration.

Heath, Edward (1916–) UK Conservative Prime Minister from 1970 to 1974. A committed pro-European, he had previously been the government Minister in charge of the UK's first application for membership.

Kohl, Helmut (1930–) Chancellor of the Federal Republic of Germany from 1982 to October 1998. A key figure in the development of the Community, he enjoyed a strong relationship with President François Mitterrand of France, though his relations with the UK Prime Minister, Margaret Thatcher, were not as positive.

Macmillan, Harold (1894–1986) UK Conservative Prime Minister from 1957 to 1963, having succeeded Anthony Eden after the Suez crisis. He advocated membership of the European Community, a policy that failed when de Gaulle vetoed the application in 1963.

Major, John (1943–) UK Conservative Prime Minister from 1990 to 1997. His period of office was marked by severe splits over the issue of European integration.

Marshall, George C. (1880–1959) US Secretary of State (1947–49) who announced a plan for the economic rehabilitation of Europe in June 1947 (Marshall Plan). This plan help to influence the European Recovery Programme and the formation of the Organisation for European Economic Cooperation (OEEC).

Mitterrand, François (1916–96) President of France from 1981 to 1985. Played a significant role in the deepening of European integration, including the development of a European single currency. Established a close relationship with the German Chancellor, Helmut Kohl.

Monnet, Jean (1888–1979) Key figure in the European integration process after 1945. Was appointed head of the French Planning Commission and his analysis highlighted the need for European nations to recover through a joint strategy. An advocate of a gradual approach to European integration, he was a significant influence behind the Schuman Plan and was appointed the first President of the High Authority of the European Coal and Steel Community.

Pompidou, Georges (1911–74) President of France from 1969 until his death in 1974. An influential figure behind the Hague summit of the Six in December 1969 which helped to foster a climate of optimism in the Community.

Prodi, Romano (1939–) President of the European Commission from 1999 until 2004 (he succeeded Jacques Santer). Prodi's Commission has not proved to be as dynamic in reforming the EU policy-making process as many would have liked.

Rey, Jean (1902–83) His period in office as President of the European Commission from 1967 to 1970 was affected by a number of factors, including the legacy of the 1965 empty chair crisis, difficulties surrounding the 1967 merger of the executives of the European Communities and Charles de Gaulle's resignation as President of France in 1969.

Santer, Jacques (1937–) President of the European Commission from 1995 to 1999. Period in office was tarnished by a March 1999 fraud report by a Committee of Independent Experts which criticised the operation of the Commission.

Schmidt, Helmut (1918–) Chancellor of the Federal Republic of Germany from 1974 to 1983. Played an important role in the development of the EEC, being one of the principal advocates of the European Monetary System that was endorsed by the European Council in 1978.

Schröder, Gerhard (1944–) Chancellor of the Federal Republic of Germany since 1998 (re-elected by a narrow majority in September 2002). His leadership of a coalition government with the Green Party since 1998 has largely been devoid of any permanent ideological bearings.

Schuman, Robert (1886–1963) The father of Europe, served as Prime Minister of France from 1947 to 1948 and Foreign Minister from 1948 to 1955. On 9 May 1950 he advanced a plan for pooling of coal and steel resources that resulted in the establishment of the European Coal and Steel Community. Served as President of the European Movement from 1955–61 and was head of the European Parliamentary Assembly from 1958–60.

Solana, Javier (1942–) Former Spanish Minister for Foreign Affairs (1992–95), he served as Secretary General of NATO (1995–99) prior to being appointed Secretary General of the Council of the European Union in October 1999 and the EU's High Representative for the Common Foreign and Security Policy (CFSP).

Spaak, Paul-Henri (1889–1972) An important figure in the furtherance of European integration who held the office of Prime Minister and Foreign Minister of Belgium on various occasions after 1945. He was influential in the creation of the Congress of Europe in 1948 and the European Movement. At the 1955 Messina Conference he was charged with the responsibility of chairing a committee that would examine proposals for a European Community (Spaak Report).

Spinelli, Altiero (1907–89) Member of the European Commission from 1970 to 1976. A strong advocate of a federal United States of Europe, he was subsequently elected a Member of the European Parliament from 1979 to 1987.

Thatcher, Margaret (1925–) UK Conservative Prime Minister from 1979 to 1990. A tough negotiating stance on the budget and her forthright personality accentuated the nation's position as an 'awkward partner'.

Thorn, Gaston (1928–) President of the European Commission from 1981–85, a period that was characterised by an absence of significant developments in the furtherance of European integration.

Tindemans, Leo (1922–) Prime Minister of Belgium 1974–78 and Foreign Minister 1981–89. Member of the European Parliament 1979–81 and 1989–99. Author of the 1975 Tindemans Report on European Union.

Trichet, Jean-Claude (1942–) Since November 2003 has held the post of President of the European Central Bank (ECB), having previously served two terms as Governor of the Bank of France.

Truman, Harry (1894–1972) President of the United States from 1945–53. Played an important role in the reconstruction of Europe, of which his key initiatives included the Truman Doctrine, the Marshall Plan and the creation of NATO.

Wilson, Harold (1916–95) UK Labour Prime Minister from 1964–70 and 1974–76. Oversaw the UK's second application for EEC membership in 1967 and in 1974 renegotiated the terms of entry that Edward Heath had obtained. In 1975 he held a referendum on Community membership.

FURTHER READING

Place of publication is London unless otherwise noted.

Websites

There are a huge number of websites devoted to the study of the EU. The most useful is the official site of the EU that can be consulted at http://www.europa.eu.int and which contains links to all of the EU institutions and areas of policy that are dealt with at the EU level. A helpful gateway to a great deal of information can be accessed by consulting the UK-based SOSIG http://www.sosig.ac.uk/eurostudies. The European Commission's Delegation to the United States provides an informative web site that includes many useful links http://www.eurunion.org/. Useful national government websites include the UK Foreign and Commonwealth Office http://www.fco.gov.uk. A full list of national governments can be found on the EU official web site at http://europa.eu.int/abc/governments/index_en.html. There are in addition a number of organisations that are devoted to the study of the EU. These include the University Association for Contemporary European Studies http://www.uaces.org/, the European Community Studies Association http://www.ecsanet.org/, and the Centre for European Policy Studies http://www.ceps.be/index.php. Research papers focusing on European integration can be accessed at European Integration On-Line Papers http://www.eiop.or.at. Other organisations that have an interest in EU affairs include The Royal Institute of International Affairs http://www.riia.org/riia, the Federal Trust http://www.fedtrust.co.uk and the Institute of European Affairs http://www/iiea.ie.

Introductory texts

There are a significant number of general introductions to the study of the EU. Among the best are Michelle Cini (ed.) *European Union Politics* (Oxford: Oxford University Press, 2003); Desmond Dinan, *Ever Closer Union* (Palgrave, 1999); John McCormick, *Understanding the European Union* (Palgrave, 2002); and Neill Nugent, *The Government and Politics of the European Union*, 5th edition (Palgrave, 2003). Those who already have a basic understanding of the EU should consult Jeremy Richardson (ed.) *European Union: Power and Policy-Making*, 2nd edition (Routledge, 2001) and Helen and William Wallace (eds) *Policy-Making in the European Union*, 4th edition (Oxford: Oxford University Press, 2000).

The sheer complexity of many of the policies and procedures that are characteristic of the EU has spawned a number of companion volumes that seek to provide answers to a range of questions. Two of the best are Timothy Bainbridge, *The Penguin Companion to the European Union* (Penguin, 1995) and Alasdair Blair, *The Longman Companion to the European Union Since 1945* (Longman, 1999). A wonderful source of information is Desmond Dinan, *An Encyclopaedia of the European Union* (Boulder,

CO: Lynne Rienner, 1998). Finally, it is often helpful to consult primary sources, of which one of the most useful compilations is Christopher Hill and Karen Smith (eds) *European Foreign Policy: Key Documents* (Routledge, 2000).

Historical survey

For general historical overviews of the EU see John Pinder, *The Building of the European Union* (Oxford: Oxford University Press, 1998) and Derek Urwin, *The Community of Europe*, 2nd edition (Longman, 1995). Andrew Moravcsik's *The Choice for Europe* (UCL Press, 1999) provides an excellent analysis of the evolution of the EU from the 1950s to the 1990s. One of the few accounts of US policy towards European integration is the excellent study by Geir Lundestad, *'Empire' by Integration* (Oxford: Oxford University Press, 1998). For an appreciation of the role played by the super-power nations of the United States and the Soviet Union in the post-war reconstruction of Europe see A.W. De Porte, *Europe Between the Superpowers*, 2nd edition (New Haven: Yale University Press, 1986).

For an analysis of the factors that were influential in promoting European unity in the post-war period see Walter Lipgens, *A History of European Integration, Vol.1, 1945–47* (Oxford: Clarendon Press, 1982); Alan Milward, *The Reconstruction of Western Europe 1945–51* (Methuen, 1984); and Ernst Haas, *The Uniting of Europe: Political, Social and Economic Forces, 1950–1957* (Stanford: Stanford University Press, 1968). Alan Milward's excellent *The European Rescue of the Nation State* sets the history of European integration within the system of European nation states after the Second World War. A personal account of the events in the postwar period is provided in Dean Acheson, *Present at the Creation* (Hamish Hamilton, 1970); François Duchene, *Jean Monnet: The First Statesman of Interdependence* (New York: Norton and Company, 1994); Paul-Henri Spaak, *The Continuing Battle: Memoirs of a European 1936–1966* (Weidenfeld & Nicolson, 1971); Jean Monnet, *Memoirs* (Collins, 1978); and Robert Marjolin, *Memoirs 1911–1986* (Weidenfeld & Nicolson, 1989). The role played by many of the individuals in the construction of Europe is discussed in Martyn Bond, Julie Smith and William Wallace (eds) *Eminent Europeans* (Greycoat Press, 1996).

Although Britain decided not to join the European Economic Community at the outset, by the 1960s there was a growing realisation that the economic benefits of membership were considerable. A refocusing of Britain's interests towards Europe is covered in Pierre Uri (ed.) *From Commonwealth to Common Market* (Penguin, 1968). In the 1960s Britain made two applications for membership, in 1963 and 1967. Both were unsuccessful. For an account of these events see Uwe Kitzinger, *The Challenge of the Common Market* (Oxford: Basil Blackwell, 1961); Uwe Kitzinger, *The Second Try* (Pergamon Press, 1968); and Georges Wilkes (ed.) *Britain's Failure to Enter the European Community 1961–63* (Frank Cass, 1997). An innovative study of European reactions to Britain's first application is provided in Piers Ludlow, *Dealing with Europe* (Cambridge: Cambridge University Press, 1997).

Just as France exercised a key role within the Community by blocking Britain's application for membership, the government that was led by General de Gaulle similarly refused to countenance any weakening in the influence of individual member states to make key decisions. This resulted in France boycotting the Community's activities in 1965, an impasse that was resolved only by the 1966 Luxembourg Compromise. For an analysis of these events see Miriam Camps, *European Unification in the Sixties* (McGraw-Hill, 1966); John Newhouse, *Collision in Brussels* (New York: Norton and Company, 1967); and John Newhouse, *De Gaulle and the Anglo-Saxons* (André Deutsch, 1970).

In 1969 Georges Pompidou succeeded de Gaulle as President of France, which helped pave the way for Britain, Denmark and Ireland to join the Community in 1973. Christopher Lord details Britain's quest for entry in *British Entry to the European Community Under the Heath Government 1970–1974* (Dartmouth: Aldershot, 1993). Subsequent enlargements of the Community resulted in the membership expanding to 12 by 1986 (Greece joined in 1981, Portugal and Spain in 1986). Enlargement of the Community was matched in the 1970s by unspectacular economic growth and an absence of strong leadership in its institutions. The fact that the Community made progress at the end of the 1970s, marked by the decision to create a European Monetary System, was greatly influenced by the efforts of the then President of the European Commission, Roy Jenkins. His personal views can be found in *European Diary 1977–1981* (Collins, 1989).

The European Monetary System proved an effective means of controlling currency fluctuations of member states throughout the 1980s. The decade was moreover notice- able for a number of important reforms that centred on the Single European Act. These included the decision to create an internal market and moves to alter methods of decision-making within the EU institutions. Many of these changes were influenced by the efforts of the President of the European Commission, Jacques Delors, and detailed accounts of his leadership can be found in Charles Grant, *Delors: Inside the House That Jacques Built* (Nicholas Brealey, 1994) and Helen Drake, *Jacques Delors* (Routledge: 2000). On the internal market see Lord Cockfield, *The European Union: Creating the Single Market* (Chichester, 1994) and Paolo Cecchini, *The European Challenge, 1992: The Benefits of a Single Market* (Aldershot: Wildwood House, 1988).

At the end of the 1980s the Community faced the important challenge of the collapse of the Soviet system of satellite states that had dominated Eastern Europe since the end of the Second World War. For a review of the cold war see John W. Young, *Cold War Europe 1945–89* (Edward Arnold, 1996) and John W. Young and John Kent, *International Relations since 1945: A Global History* (Oxford: Oxford University Press, 2004) . An excellent account of the key issues in the post-cold war period can be found in Robin Niblett and William Wallace (eds) *Rethinking European Order* (Palgrave, 2001) and Ian Clark, *The Post-Cold War Order* (Oxford: Oxford University Press, 2001). Changes to the geopolitical order of Europe had a bearing on the outcome of the 1993 Maastricht Treaty on European Union. For a review of the Maastricht negotiations see Richard Corbett, *The Treaty of Maastricht* (Longman, 1993). The position of Britain is charted in Anthony Forster, *Britain and the Maastricht Negotiations* (Macmillan, 1999) and Alasdair Blair, *Dealing with Europe* (Aldershot: Ashgate, 1999). A useful text that examines the challenges of the 'new Europe' is Jack Hayward and Edward Page (eds) *Governing the New Europe* (Cambridge: Polity Press, 1995). One impact of the Maastricht Treaty was to establish intergovernmental pillars in the EU for cooperation in the fields of Common Foreign and Security Policy and Justice and Home Affairs. A standard text on the intergovernmental pillars is Eileen Denza, *The Intergovernmental Pillars of the European Union* (Oxford: Oxford University Press, 2002). Despite the significant reforms that were brought about by the Maastricht Treaty, including the creation of a single currency, further changes to the structure and workings of the EU were set out in the Amsterdam and Nice Treaties. On the Amsterdam Treaty see Nanette Neuwahl, Philip Lynch and Wyn Rees (eds) *Reforming the European Union* (Longman, 1999) and Martin Westlake, *The European Union Beyond Amsterdam* (Routledge, 1998). On the Nice Treaty see Kim Feus (ed.) *The Treaty of Nice Explained* (Kogan Page/The Federal Trust, 2001) and David Galloway, *The Treaty of Nice and Beyond* (Sheffield: Sheffield Academic Press, 2001).

European institutions

A key area of interest for many scholars in recent years has been the institutions of the EU. Some of the best books that are focused on the EU institutions are John Peterson and Michael Shackleton (eds) *The Institutions of the European Union* (Oxford: Oxford University Press, 2002); John Peterson and Elizabeth Bomberg, *Decision-Making in the European Union* (Palgrave, 1999); and Simon Hix, *The Political System of the European Union* (Palgrave, 1999). An accessible introduction to the EU institutions is Alex Warleigh (ed.) *Understanding European Union Institutions* (Routledge, 2002). For a review of the role of the European Commission see Michelle Cini, *The European Commission* (Manchester: Manchester University Press, 1996); Liesbet Hooghe, *The European Commission and the Integration of Europe* (Cambridge: Cambridge University Press, 2001); and Neill Nugent, *The European Commission* (Palgrave, 2001). The increased powers that have been attributed to the European Parliament are covered in Richard Corbett, Francis Jacobs and Michael Shackleton, *The European Parliament*, 4th edition (John Harper, 2000) and Julie Smith, *Europe's Elected Parliament* (Sheffield: Sheffield Academic Press, 1999). An important study of the party group system within the European Parliament can be found in Amy Kreppel, *The European Parliament and the Supranational Party System* (Cambridge: Cambridge University Press, 2002). For a review of the Council of Ministers see Fiona Hayes-Renshaw and Helen Wallace, *The Council of Ministers* (Palgrave, 1997); Philippa Sherrington, *The Council of Ministers* (Pinter, 2000); and John Peterson and Elizabeth Bomberg, *Decision-Making in the European Union* (Macmillan, 1999). Good discussion of the European Court of Justice's role can be found in Renaud Dehousse, *The European Court of Justice* (Palgrave, 1998) and L. Neville Brown and Tom Kennedy, *The Court of Justice of the European Communities*, 5th edition (Sweet and Maxwell, 2000). The complex legal system of the EU is examined by Josephine Shaw, *Law of the European Union*, 3rd edition (Palgrave, 2000). Finally, the relationship between national courts and the Court of Justice is examined in Karen Alter, *Establishing the Supremacy of European Law* (Oxford: Oxford University Press, 2001).

Policy areas

Since the foundations of the Treaties of Rome the EU's competence has spread to include a whole range of policies that were previously considered to be purely the priority of member states. On agricultural policy see Robert Ackrill, *The Common Agricultural Policy* (Sheffield: Sheffield Academic Press, 2000). For environmental policy see John McCormick, *Environmental Policy in the European Union* (Palgrave, 2001). Energy policy is covered in Jane Matláry, *Energy Policy in the European Union* (Macmillan, 1997). Competition policy is analysed by Michelle Cini and Lee McGowan, *Competition Policy in the European Union* (Macmillan, 1998). On technology policy see John Peterson and Margaret Sharp, *Technology Policy in the European Union* (Macmillan, 1998). For a review of social policy see Linda Hantrais, *Social Policy in the European Union*, 2nd edition (Macmillan, 2000). The Single European Market is discussed in Kenneth Armstrong and Simon Bulmer, *The Governance of the Single European Market* (Manchester: Manchester University Press, 1998).

A notable area of change has been in the EU's foreign policy capability and good overviews of this subject can be found in John Peterson and Helen Sjursen, *A Common Foreign Policy for Europe?* (Routledge, 1998); Hazel Smith, *European Foreign Policy* (Pluto Press, 2002); and Brian White, *Understanding European Foreign Policy* (Palgrave, 2001). The broader remit of the EU's external relations policy is discussed in Roy Ginsberg, *The European Union in International Politics* (Boulder, CO: Rowman and Littlefield, 2001); and John Bretherton and Charlotte Vogler, *The European Union as a Global Actor* (Routledge, 1999). Matters relating to justice and homes affairs are covered in Andrew Geddes, *Immigration and European Integration* (Manchester: Manchester University Press, 2000). The EU's relations with the third world are covered in Martin Holland, *The European Union and the Third World*, (Palgrave, 2002). The enlargement of the EU is tackled in Michael Baun, *A Wider Europe: The Process and Politics of European Union Enlargement* (Oxford: Rowman and Littlefield, 2000); and Graham Avery and Fraser Cameron, *The Enlargement of the European Union* (Sheffield: Sheffield Academic Press, 1999).

One of the most topical subjects in the EU today is monetary union. The politics surrounding the negotiation of monetary union in the Maastricht Treaty is tackled in Kenneth Dyson and Kevin Featherstone, *The Road to Maastricht* (Oxford: Oxford University Press, 1999). Good analysis of EMU can be found in Malcolm Levitt and Christopher Lord, *The Political Economy of Monetary Union* (Macmillan, 2000). For a discussion of Britain's negotiating position on monetary union see Alasdair Blair, *Saving the Pound?* (Prentice Hall, 2002).

A cumulative effect of the growth in the number of EU policies and the fact that they intrude into virtually every area of domestic policy has been that they have impacted on the ways in which government operates within member states. This state of affairs is referred to as a process of Europeanisation and some of the most useful sources on this subject include Christoph Knill, *The Europeanisation of National Administrations* (Cambridge: Cambridge University Press, 2001); Klaus Goetz and Simon Hix, *Europeanised Politics?* (Frank Cass, 2001); and Martha Green Cowles, James Caporaso and Thomas Risse (eds) *Transforming Europe*, Ithaca: Cornell University Press, 2001).

Some commentators consider there is insufficient democracy within the EU and for an understanding of this subject see David Beetham and Christopher Lord, *Legitimacy in the European Union* (Longman, 1996); Dimitris Chryssochoou, *Democracy in the European Union* (I.B. Taurus, 2000); and Michael Newman, *Democracy, Sovereignty and the European Union* (Hurst, 1996). In attempting to reflect the interests of the different regions of the EU, a strong regional policy has emerged. Analysis of this can be found in Ian Bache, *The Politics of European Union Regional Policy* (Sheffield: Sheffield Academic Press, 1999); Liesbet Hooghe (ed.) *Cohesion Policy and European Integration* (Oxford: Oxford University Press, 1996); and Michael Keating, *New Regionalism in Western Europe* (Cheltenham: Edward Elgar, 2000).

Theoretical and conceptual accounts

Important works which provide an overview of integration theory are Dimitris Chryssochoou, *Theorizing European Integration* (Sage, 2001) and Ben Rosamond,

Theories of European Integration (Macmillan, 2000). Federalist accounts can be found in Michael Burgess, *Federalism and the European Union* (Routledge, 2000). An introduction to intergovernmentalism can be found in Stanley Hoffman, *The European Sisyphus* (Oxford: Westview Press, 1995) and Andrew Moravcsik, *The Choice for Europe* (University College London Press, 1998). Constructivism offers a new approach to the study of European integration, of which the most useful text is Thomas Christiansen, Knud Erik Jørgensen and Antje Wiener (eds) *The Social Construction of* Europe (Sage, 2001). Simon Hix has argued that the EU is best understood from the angle of comparative politics in *The Political System of the European Union* (Macmillan, 1999). A multi-level governance approach can be found in Liesbet Hooghe and Gary Marks, *Multi-level Governance and European Integration* (Boulder, Colo.: Rowman and Littlefield, 2001). Finally, for an institutionalist viewpoint see Gerhard Schneider and Mark Aspinwall (eds), *The Rules of Integration* (Manchester: Manchester University Press, 2001). By far the majority of the work that has been written on integration theory has appeared in academic journals and there are a number of readers which bring these articles into a collective publication, including Michael O'Neill, *The Politics of European Integration* (Routledge, 1996) and Brent Nelson and Alexander Stubb (eds) *The European Union*, 2nd edition (Macmillan, 1998).

REFERENCES

The place of publication is London unless otherwise noted.

Cecchini, P., Catinat, M. and Jacquemin, A. (1988) *The European Challenge: 1992: The Benefits of a Single Market*, Aldershot: Wildwood House.

Cockfield, Lord Arthur (1994) *The European Union: Creating the Single Market*, Wiley Chancery.

Denman, R. (1996) *Missed Chances: Britain and Europe in the Twentieth Century*, Cassell.

Dinan, D. (1999) *Ever Closer Union? An Introduction to the European Community*, Macmillan, 2nd edition.

Duchêne, F. (1996) 'Jean Monnet – Pragmatic Visionary' in Martyn Bond, Julie Smith and William Wallace (eds) *Eminent Europeans*, The Greycoat Press, pp.45–61.

Haas, E.B. (1968) *The Uniting of Europe: Political, Social and Economic Forces 1950–57*, Stevens, 2nd edition.

Hallstein, W. (1962) *United Europe: Challenges and Opportunity*, Oxford University Press.

Heath, E. (1998) *The Course of My Life*, Hodder & Stoughton.

Henderson, N. (1994) *Mandarin: The Diaries of an Ambassador 1969–1982*, Weidenfeld & Nicolson.

Henig, S. (2002) *The Uniting of Europe*, Routledge, 2nd edition.

Hix, S. (1999) *The Political System of the European Union*, Palgrave.

Jenkins, R. (1989) *European Diary, 1977–1981*, Collins.

Jenkins, R. (1991) *A Life at the Centre*, Macmillan.

Macmillan, H. (1973) *At the End of the Day, 1961–63*, Macmillan.

Marjolin, R. *et al.* (1975) *Report of the Study Group Economic Monetary Union 1980, 'Marjolin Report'*, Brussels: Commission of the European Communities.

May, A. (1999) *Britain and Europe since 1945*, Longman.

Milward, A. (1984) *The Reconstruction of Western Europe 1945–1951*, Methuen & Co. Ltd.

Milward, A. (1992) *The European Rescue of the Nation State*, Routledge and Kegan & Paul.

Milward, A. and Brennan, G. (1996) *Britain's Place in the World: A Historical Enquiry into Import Controls 1945–1960*, Routledge.

Mitrany, D. (1946) *A Working Peace System*, Royal Institute of International Affairs.

Monnet, J. (1978) *Memoirs* (translated by R. Mayne), New York: Doubleday & Company.

Padoa-Schioppa, T. (1987) *Efficiency, Stability and Equity: A Strategy for the Evolution of the Economic System of the EC*, Oxford: Oxford University Press.

Paterson, W.E. (1994) 'The Chancellor and Foreign Policy' in Stephen Padgett (ed.) *The Development of the German Chancellorship: Adenauer to Kohl*, Hurst & Company.

Reynolds, D. (2000) *Britannia Overruled*, Longman.

Schmidt, H. (1985) *A Grand Strategy for the West*, Henry L. Stimson Lectures, Yale University, Yale University Press.

Spaak, P.-H. (1971) *The Continuing Battle: Memoirs of a European 1936–1966*, Weidenfeld & Nicolson.

Thatcher, M. (1993) *The Downing Street Years*, HarperCollins.

Willis, F. (1968) *France, Germany and the New Europe 1945–1963*, Stanford: Stanford University Press.

Young, J.W. (1991) *Cold War Europe 1945–1989: A Political History*, Edward Arnold.

Young, J.W. (2000) *Britain and European Unity 1945–1999*, 2nd edition, Macmillan.

INDEX

General Editors: Clive Emsley & Gordon Martel

The series was founded by Patrick Richardson in 1966. Between 1980 and 1996 Roger Lockyer edited the series before handing over to Clive Emsley (Professor of History at the Open University) and Gordon Martel (Professor of International History at the University of Northern British Columbia, Canada and Senior Research Fellow at De Montfort University).

MEDIEVAL ENGLAND

The Pre-Reformation Church in England 1400–1530 (Second edition)
Christopher Harper-Bill   0 582 28989 0

Lancastrians and Yorkists: The Wars of the Roses
David R. Cook   0 582 35384 X

Family and Kinship in England 1450–1800
Will Coster   0 582 35717 9

TUDOR ENGLAND

Henry VII (Third edition)
Roger Lockyer & Andrew Thrush   0 582 20912 9

Henry VIII (Second edition)
M. D. Palmer   0 582 35437 4

Tudor Rebellions (Fourth edition)
Anthony Fletcher & Diarmaid MacCulloch   0 582 28990 4

The Reign of Mary I (Second edition)
Robert Tittler   0 582 06107 5

Early Tudor Parliaments 1485–1558
Michael A. R. Graves   0 582 03497 3

The English Reformation 1530–1570
W. J. Sheils   0 582 35398 X

Elizabethan Parliaments 1559–1601 (Second edition)
Michael A. R. Graves   0 582 29196 8

England and Europe 1485–1603 (Second edition)
Susan Doran   0 582 28991 2

The Church of England 1570–1640
Andrew Foster   0 582 35574 5

STUART BRITAIN

Social Change and Continuity: England 1550–1750 (Second edition)
Barry Coward   0 582 29442 8

James I (Second edition)
S. J. Houston   0 582 20911 0

The English Civil War 1640–1649
Martyn Bennett   0 582 35392 0

Charles I, 1625–1640
Brian Quintrell   0 582 00354 7

The English Republic 1649–1660 (Second edition)
Toby Barnard   0 582 08003 7

Radical Puritans in England 1550–1660
R. J. Acheson   0 582 35515 X

The Restoration and the England of Charles II (Second edition)
John Miller   0 582 29223 9

The Glorious Revolution (Second edition)
John Miller   0 582 29222 0

EARLY MODERN EUROPE

The Renaissance (Second edition)
Alison Brown   0 582 30781 3

The Emperor Charles V
Martyn Rady   0 582 35475 7

French Renaissance Monarchy: Francis I and Henry II (Second edition)
Robert Knecht   0 582 28707 3

The Protestant Reformation in Europe
Andrew Johnston   0 582 07020 1

The French Wars of Religion 1559–1598 (Second edition)
Robert Knecht   0 582 28533 X

Phillip II
Geoffrey Woodward   0 582 07232 8

The Thirty Years' War
Peter Limm   0 582 35373 4

Louis XIV
Peter Campbell   0 582 01770 X

Spain in the Seventeenth Century
Graham Darby   0 582 07234 4

Peter the Great
William Marshall   0 582 00355 5

EUROPE 1789–1918

Britain and the French Revolution
Clive Emsley   0 582 36961 4

Revolution and Terror in France 1789–1795 (Second edition)
D. G. Wright   0 582 00379 2

Napoleon and Europe
D. G. Wright   0 582 35457 9

The Abolition of Serfdom in Russia 1762–1907
David Moon   0 582 29486 X

Nineteenth-Century Russia: Opposition to Autocracy
Derek Offord   0 582 35767 5

The Constitutional Monarchy in France 1814–48
Pamela Pilbeam   0 582 31210 8

The 1848 Revolutions (Second edition)
Peter Jones   0 582 06106 7

The Italian Risorgimento
M. Clark   0 582 00353 9

Bismarck & Germany 1862–1890 (Second edition)
D. G. Williamson   0 582 29321 9

Imperial Germany 1890–1918
Ian Porter, Ian Armour and Roger Lockyer   0 582 03496 5

The Dissolution of the Austro-Hungarian Empire 1867–1918 (Second edition)
John W. Mason   0 582 29466 5

Second Empire and Commune: France 1848–1871 (Second edition)
William H. C. Smith   0 582 28705 7

France 1870–1914 (Second edition)
Robert Gildea   0 582 29221 2

The Scramble for Africa (Second edition)
M. E. Chamberlain   0 582 36881 2

Late Imperial Russia 1890–1917
John F. Hutchinson   0 582 32721 0

The First World War
Stuart Robson   0 582 31556 5

Austria, Prussia and Germany 1806–1871
John Breuilly   0 582 43739 3

Napoleon: Conquest, Reform and Reorganisation
Clive Emsley   0 582 43795 4

The French Revolution 1787–1804
Peter Jones   0 582 77289 3

The Origins of the First World War (Third edition)
Gordon Martel   0 582 43804 7

The Birth of Industrial Britain
Kenneth Morgan   0 582 30270 6

EUROPE SINCE 1918

The Russian Revolution (Second edition)
Anthony Wood   0 582 35559 1

Lenin's Revolution: Russia 1917–1921
David Marples   0 582 31917 X

Stalin and Stalinism (Third edition)
Martin McCauley   0 582 50587 9

The Weimar Republic (Second edition)
John Hiden   0 582 28706 5

The Inter-War Crisis 1919–1939
Richard Overy   0 582 35379 3

Fascism and the Right in Europe 1919–1945
Martin Blinkhorn   0 582 07021 X

Spain's Civil War (Second edition)
Harry Browne   0 582 28988 2

The Third Reich (Third edition)
D. G. Williamson   0 582 20914 5

The Origins of the Second World War (Second edition)
R. J. Overy   0 582 29085 6

The Second World War in Europe
Paul MacKenzie   0 582 32692 3

The French at War 1934–1944
Nicholas Atkin   0 582 36899 5

Anti-Semitism before the Holocaust
Albert S. Lindemann   0 582 36964 9

The Holocaust: The Third Reich and the Jews
David Engel   0 582 32720 2

Germany from Defeat to Partition 1945–1963
D. G. Williamson   0 582 29218 2

Britain and Europe since 1945
Alex May   0 582 30778 3

Eastern Europe 1945–1969: From Stalinism to Stagnation
Ben Fowkes   0 582 32693 1

Eastern Europe since 1970
Bülent Gökay   0 582 32858 6

The Khrushchev Era 1953–1964
Martin McCauley   0 582 27776 0

Hitler and the Rise of the Nazi Party *Frank McDonough*	0 582 50606 9
The Soviet Union Under Brezhnev *William Tompson*	0 582 32719 9
The European Union since 1945 *Alasdair Blair*	0 582 42393 7

NINETEENTH-CENTURY BRITAIN

Britain before the Reform Acts: Politics and Society 1815–1832 *Eric J. Evans*	0 582 00265 6
Parliamentary Reform in Britain c. 1770–1918 *Eric J. Evans*	0 582 29467 3
Democracy and Reform 1815–1885 *D. G. Wright*	0 582 31400 3
Poverty and Poor Law Reform in Nineteenth-Century Britain 1834–1914: From Chadwick to Booth *David Englander*	0 582 31554 9
The Birth of Industrial Britain: Economic Change 1750–1850 *Kenneth Morgan*	0 582 29833 4
Chartism (Third edition) *Edward Royle*	0 582 29080 5
Peel and the Conservative Party 1830–1850 *Paul Adelman*	0 582 35557 5
Gladstone, Disraeli and later Victorian Politics (Third edition) *Paul Adelman*	0 582 29322 7
Britain and Ireland: From Home Rule to Independence *Jeremy Smith*	0 582 30193 9

TWENTIETH-CENTURY BRITAIN

The Rise of the Labour Party 1880–1945 (Third edition) *Paul Adelman*	0 582 29210 7
The Conservative Party and British Politics 1902–1951 *Stuart Ball*	0 582 08002 9
The Decline of the Liberal Party 1910–1931 (Second edition) *Paul Adelman*	0 582 27733 7
The British Women's Suffrage Campaign 1866–1928 *Harold L. Smith*	0 582 29811 3

War & Society in Britain 1899–1948
Rex Pope   0 582 03531 7

The British Economy since 1914: A Study in Decline?
Rex Pope   0 582 30194 7

Unemployment in Britain between the Wars
Stephen Constantine   0 582 35232 0

The Attlee Governments 1945–1951
Kevin Jefferys   0 582 06105 9

The Conservative Governments 1951–1964
Andrew Boxer   0 582 20913 7

Britain under Thatcher
Anthony Seldon and Daniel Collings   0 582 31714 2

Britain and Empire 1880–1945
Dane Kennedy   0 582 41493 8

INTERNATIONAL HISTORY

The Eastern Question 1774–1923 (Second edition)
A. L. Macfie   0 582 29195 X

India 1885–1947: The Unmaking of an Empire
Ian Copland   0 582 38173 8

The United States and the First World War
Jennifer D. Keene   0 582 35620 2

Women and the First World War
Susan R. Grayzel   0 582 41876 3

Anti-Semitism before the Holocaust
Albert S. Lindemann   0 582 36964 9

The Origins of the Cold War 1941–1949 (Third edition)
Martin McCauley   0 582 77284 2

Russia, America and the Cold War 1949–1991 (Second edition)
Martin McCauley   0 582 78482 4

The Arab–Israeli Conflict
Kirsten E. Schulze   0 582 31646 4

The United Nations since 1945: Peacekeeping and the Cold War
Norrie MacQueen   0 582 35673 3

Decolonisation: The British Experience since 1945
Nicholas J. White   0 582 29087 2

The Collapse of the Soviet Union
David R. Marples   0 582 50599 2

WORLD HISTORY

China in Transformation 1900–1949
Colin Mackerras   0 582 31209 4

Japan Faces the World 1925–1952
Mary L. Hanneman   0 582 36898 7

Japan in Transformation 1952–2000
Jeff Kingston   0 582 41875 5

China since 1949
Linda Benson   0 582 35722 5

South Africa: The Rise and Fall of Apartheid
Nancy L. Clark and William H. Worger   0 582 41437 7

Race and Empire
Jane Samson   0 582 41837 2

US HISTORY

American Abolitionists
Stanley Harrold   0 582 35738 1

The American Civil War 1861–1865
Reid Mitchell   0 582 31973 0

America in the Progressive Era 1890–1914
Lewis L. Gould   0 582 35671 7

The United States and the First World War
Jennifer D. Keene   0 582 35620 2

The Truman Years 1945–1953
Mark S. Byrnes   0 582 32904 3

The Korean War
Steven Hugh Lee   0 582 31988 9

The Origins of the Vietnam War
Fredrik Logevall   0 582 31918 8

The Vietnam War
Mitchell Hall   0 582 32859 4

American Expansionism 1783–1860
Mark S. Joy   0 582 36965 7

The United States and Europe in the Twentieth Century
David Ryan   0 582 30864 X

The Civil Rights Movement
Bruce J. Dierenfield   0 582 35737 3